LESSONS FROM THE CRAFT

Seeing God in Masonic Rituals

Dr. Douglas Reece

Lessons From the Craft: Seeing God in Masonic Rituals
Copyright © 2022 by Dr. Douglas Reece and Perfect Ashlar Publishing.
All Right Reserved.

All rights reserved. No part of this publication may be reproduced, distributed, or transmitted in any form or by any means, including photocopying, recording, or other electronic or mechanical methods, without the prior written permission of the publisher or author, except in the case of brief quotations embodied in critical reviews and certain other noncommercial uses permitted by copyright law. For permission requests, email to the publisher, addressed "Attention: Permissions Coordinator," at the email address below.

PerfectAshlarPublishing@gmail.com

Perfect Ashlar Publishing

Universal City, TX

For ordering information please visit Perfect Ashlar Publishing's website at:
www.PerfectAshlarPublishing.com

LESSONS FROM THE CRAFT

Table of Contents

Introduction 1
Chapter 1 5
    Christian Origins
Chapter 2 15
    Our Hidden Masonic Resource
Chapter 3 21
    Masonic Charity
Chapter 4 35
    The Plumb Line
Chapter 5 39
    The Wooden Bowl
Chapter 6 45
    Subdue the Passions
Chapter 7 51
    Justice and Judgement
Chapter 8 59
    Untempered Mortar
Chapter 9 65
    Squaring Our Actions
Chapter 10 71
    Why by the Square?
Chapter 11 79
    The Masonic Blue Slipper
Chapter 12 85
    The Tabernacle
Chapter 13 91
    The Words We Use
Chapter 14 95
    The Lion of the Tribe of Judah
Chapter 15 101
    Who Wrote This Stuff?

Chapter 16 107
   Boaz and Jachin
Chapter 17 113
   Why Are So Many Masons Bored with The Bible?
Chapter 18 117
   In The Beginning God…
Chapter 19 127
   Why did your man join the Masons?
Chapter 20 135
   Sacrifices
Chapter 21 139
   Anchor and Ark
Chapter 22 143
   How Different Are we?
Chapter 23 149
   Just how We've Always Done It
Chapter 24 153
   The Lambskin Apron
Chapter 25 159
   Are There Missing Stones in Masonry?
Chapter 26 165
   Matthew 7:7 Ask, Seek, and Knock
Chapter 27 173
   Jacobs Ladder
Chapter 28 179
   A Certain Point
Chapter 29 183
   Living Stones
Chapter 30 187
   Measurement of the Temple
About the Author 193

INTRODUCTION

Coffee steam winds its way up the spiral staircase to heaven's gate. A cool spring morning breeze brings fresh thoughts of praise and adoration for the creation God has given us. A walk in the woods surrounding the house allows me time to talk with God and His Son. What a wonderful time. The deer are playing in the clearing, and the birds are darting in and out of the sun's rays peeking through the trees. I look out across the meadow, and a thought strikes me, "what have we been teaching our brethren?'

Are the lessons within the fraternity lost, or have we just lost our desire to pass along those critical life lessons our forefathers have so graciously given us? "Father, what will happen to this great fraternity if we forget what our ancestors were teaching?" Sitting on the bench of the picnic table, I waited for God's response.

Silence. Silence so loud, your soul screams in agony for His response.

There, in the midst of this silence, was God's answer. Like the cries of the Jewish people in ancient Israel during the captivities and after returning home, we have been created with free will.

We were created with a power to choose action or to sit and wait for God to motivate us to greatness. God laid down his desires for His people as testified by the writings of the prophets. Our fraternity has some of the best practical lessons of life contained with the ceremonies of our ritual. The Appendant Bodies also have great teachings which expound the great moral and religious lessons contained with the New Testament and the Old Testament. A question arises, "Have we been guilty of keeping those lessons a secret so long that we have lost what was taught in our past?" The fraternity as a whole has an abundance of historians. Masonic education in most lodges and OES chapters today centers around history. Without a doubt, we should remember our history and keep those memories alive; however, in our endeavors we have failed to convey the reason behind such a rich history. Have we failed to live up to our motto of making good men better? Watching two squirrels swirling around the trunk of the old oak tree chasing each other's tails, I was reminded that we could be chasing our own tails.

Remembering conversations in the past with several Past Grand Masters, I thought about a common theme they communicated. In essence, we could not teach a specific religion or slant our teaching towards one religion. We could not risk offending someone for fear of a lawsuit. We have to be politically correct. Does this mean we have to be so correct that we lose our identity? Does this correctness demand that our forefather's efforts now will go in vain, and we will lose this fraternity to the withering sands of time into nothingness?

Our heritage demands action. Our founding fathers were men of action. Making a stand for what is right in the All-Seeing Eye of God, not in the eyes of man. We are a private organization which demands members of sound moral character. If such is our heritage, why then have we succumbed to being as pliable as putty? As the smoke from my pipe rises and swirls in the breeze, God's gentle nudge reminds me that it is also our duty to obey the laws of those who govern us along with His laws. Thoughts and teaching of those mentors who molded numerous masons filled my mind with such clarity I felt as if they were talking with me again. I turned when I saw the lone buck, so majestic; look me squarely in the eye as if to convey the message of our forefathers to take the action needed. Present the instruction as I was presented the instruction. It is up to them to accept or reject it, depending on their religious preference.

That is how it was presented to me; "Here's what we think it means; the rest is up to you." In those days, not that long ago, like the early 1970s, as we learned our masonic ritual, the mentors who were teaching it would explain what they felt the meaning should be. They would explain how it applied to our lives in a practical manner and what the brotherhood of masonry is all about from a Christian point of view. I even had one mentor in St. Louis who was Jewish, and the conversations we had were quite fulfilling.

He would shed light on the Temple and ceremonies, the customs of the times, and an explanation of the scriptural references from the Jewish point of view. I walked and talked with the Father until the coffee in the mug got cold. It was then that I felt the Spirit of God telling me what direction to head. So, I turned toward the creek to the south. When I tripped over a branch because I wasn't paying a bit of attention to where I was walking, He gently reminded me that was not what He meant and that I needed to start my ministry and write down the lessons I have learned for the benefit of the brethren now and in the future. So, with that injunction of the Holy Spirit, I write for you what I have been taught throughout my search for Christ in the Masonic Ritual. I have consulted only those in the United States for the present, as I realize that European rituals are different and have different observances and meanings.

May you find the lessons, revelations, meanings, and explanations contained within these pages inspiring enough to start your own masonic quest for knowledge and meaning.

Doug Reece

CHAPTER 1
Christian Origins

Freemasonry, as we know it in the United States, started with the colonization of America.

However, we discover from the very beginning Freemasonry was intended as a Christian institution, and its symbols, degrees, and ceremonies were all interpreted according to fundamental Christian doctrines.

Our founding fathers of Masonry were not pagans, cultists, occultists, Mayans, druids, witches, Hindus, or Buddhists, according to their personal views, with maybe the exception of Albert Pike. They did not claim that Masonry descended from ancient mystery cults or the worship of Isis. Few, if any, knew nothing of such ideas.

In his book "The Truth About Masons, Robert Morey states," "The Christian interpretation of Freemasonry was the accepted norm until the latter half of the nineteenth century.

All the early writers were committed Christians, and many were clergymen of conservative churches. A Christian view of the origin of the Lodge was given by Anderson, Hutchinson, Oliver, Webb, Lyon, Hughan, and many others." (page 27)

Hutchinson described an evangelical description of Masonry. He referred to Jesus Christ in the following words in the third degree.

"The great Father of All, commiserating the miseries of the world, sent His only Son, who was innocence itself, to teach the doctrine of Salvation, by whom man was raised from the death of sin unto the life of righteousness; from the tomb of corruption unto the chambers of hope; from the darkness of despair to the celestial beams of faith. Thus the Master Mason represents a man under the Christian doctrine saved from the grave of iniquity and raised to the faith, and since we are raised from the state of corruption, we bear the emblem of the Holy Trinity as the insignia of our vows and of the origin of the Master's order." Mackey comments: "The Christianization of the third or Master's degree, that is, the interpretation of its symbols as referring to Christ and to Christian dogmas, is not peculiar to nor original with Hutchinson. It was the accepted doctrine of almost all his contemporaries, and several of the rituals of the eighteenth century contain unmistakable traces of it."[1]

Mackey further comments; "Even as late as the middle of the nineteenth century, Dr. Oliver had explicitly declared that if he had not been fully convinced that Freemasonry is a system of Christian Ethics – that it contributes its aid to point the way to the Grand Lodge above, through the Cross of Christ – he should never have been found among the number of its advocates. The interpretation of the symbols of Freemasonry from a Christian point of view was, therefore, at the period when Hutchinson advanced his theory, neither novel to the Craft nor peculiar to him."[2]

Dr. Oliver's position was clear according to what Mackey quoted from him, "The conclusion is therefore obvious. If the lectures of Freemasonry refer only to events which preceded the advent of

---

[1] Albert Mackey, History of Freemasonry (New York: Masonic History Co., 1898, I:136
[2] Ibid, I:137

Christ, and if those events which consist exclusively of admitted types of the Great Deliverer, who was preordained to become a voluntary sacrifice for the salvation of mankind, it will clearly follow that the Order was originally instituted in accordance with the true principles of the Christian Religion." (Ibid I:149)

According to Mackey, on page 147, "the first attempt to de-Christianize the Craft was by Hemming in 1813". Masonry in general rejected Hemming's attempt to "de-Christianize" the Craft. The Norton affair is an example of the Christian nature of early Masonry. It was not, until the anti-Masonic movement from 1826 – 1836; when conservative Christians were forced out of freemasonry and that the processes of de-Christianizing and paganizing the Craft could get underway.

In line with the anti-Masonic hysteria of the period following the murder of Captain Morgan, church leaders like Charles Finney, D.L. Moody, Charles Blanchard, Alexander Campbell, and R.A. Torrey managed to extract nearly all of the evangelical Christians out of Freemasonry using scriptural references out of context.

Many conservative churches gave their Masonic members an ultimatum that they had to quit Masonry or get out of the church. As a result, families, churches, and close friendships were torn into pieces as the controversy tore through the country from one end to the other.

This kind of pressure through the churches caused the shut down over half of the Lodges in the country.

The churches even managed to shut down every single lodge in the state of Vermont! This ultimatum from the churches caused the

Christian majority of the lodge to leave the Craft. As conservative Christians left Freemasonry, it gave the members who did not care what the Christian church or its leaders had to say the opportunity to seize power within local lodges. The vast majority of the Masons who assumed leadership positions after the anti-Masonic purges began to reinterpret the Craft according to anti-Christian principles. Albert Pike stated in Morals and Dogma on page 814 that, "The best friends of Masonry in America were the anti-Masons of 1826" because they "purified Masonry by persecution."[3] Pike believed the anti-Masonic movement drove the Christian majority out of the Lodge which paved the way clear for him to redesign the entire Craft (at least the what is now the Scottish Rite) according to his own pagan religious views. Pike, because of his earlier episodes in Catholic Seminary and consequent expulsion, expressed nothing but contempt for historic and contemporary Christian interpreters of Freemasonry, and singled out Webb and Preston for this special ridicule. If anyone thought he did not understand the historic Christian view of Masonry, he would describe it in great detail and then dismissed it with the wave of his hand.

If we study the history from 1723 on, especially in the formation of the Grand Lodge of England and the colonization of America, Freemasonry was understood to be a Christian institution until the anti-Masonic movement began in 1826.

In 1871, Pike tried but failed to free Masonry from its Christian heritage. His Pagan views were ignored by most in his day. An

---

[3] Morals and Dogma of the Ancient and Accepted Scottish Rite, Supreme Council of the 33rd Degree, 1928 edition.

avalanche of Masonic books that sought to trace Masonry to pagan origins fueled his attempts to paganize the Craft and did not start until the 1920s. I want to point out that the pagan interpretation of the Craft was, for the most part, limited to leadership. Pike's book, Morals and Dogmas is so poorly written that very few Masons own a copy of it or have even read it.

During the same 1920s, when the leadership was becoming pagan in its views of the Craft, millions of conservative Christians flooded back into Freemasonry. One example would be the hundreds of thousands of conservative Southern Baptists who joined the Fraternity. During this time, the Craft recorded its highest growth in membership in its history.

Since many of these new members were pastors, elders, and deacons in their churches, they naturally picked up the original Christian interpretation of the symbols and rites of Freemasonry. Thus, while the leadership was becoming pagan, the bulk of the membership returned to the original Christian view.

Since the 1920s, Freemasonry has developed along two different tracks. For the vast majority, the Craft is a fraternity and not a religion.

In particular, it is not some kind of pagan religion that would contradict Christian convictions. This is why many members feel insulted when a modern anti-Mason calls them druids or witches. On the other hand, a small vocal minority openly calls Freemasonry a religion and dogmatically states that Masonry is a revival of certain ancient pagan religions that are all openly anti-Christian.

Since they are constantly writing books on Freemasonry, which give it a pagan slant, and they arrogantly claim to speak for the whole Fraternity, is it any wonder that anti-Masons have a field day with their extreme statements? In many of their books, modern pagan writers such as Manly Hall do not hesitate to castigate the vast Christian majority of the Craft as "stupid" and "ignorant." There is clearly a civil war going on within Freemasonry itself that must be resolved one way or the other.

The tension in the Lodge between the pagans and the Christians has resulted in a tremendous decline in attendance and membership. This tension is, in reality, a fight over whose religious convictions will be allowed to interpret the symbols and rites of the Craft. For example, does the Masonic triangle still represent the Christian Trinity of the Father, Son, and Holy Spirit as the founders of Freemasonry believed, or does it now represent the Hindu trinity of Krishna, Shiva, and Brahma as claimed by the modern pagan writers? It is evident to anyone that the conflict is irrefutably religious in nature.

The persistence of the Christian interpretation explains why millions of sincere Christians presently belong to the Craft and do not see any conflict between it and their Christian convictions. They do not believe in the new pagan interpretation of Freemasonry and continue to believe in the historic Christian interpretation of the Craft. They represent the "silent" majority of Freemasonry.

Pre-biblical Origins

Early Masons such as Anderson, Hutchinson, and Oliver attempted to give Freemasonry an aura of antiquity by tracing its beginnings to pre-biblical times. Since the symbols of Freemasonry illustrate God's plans of salvation through the saving work of Jesus Christ, Freemasonry began in the eternal decrees of God before the foundation of the world.

They held that Freemasonry was also a part of the original religion of all humanity, which God revealed to Adam in the Garden. It was a monotheistic religion that reflected the values and truths later revealed in Scripture. This is why the first Landmark is to believe in only one god. Pagan religions are a corruption of this original religion.

Paganism, with its many gods, is thus a falling away from the monotheistic biblical religion and from Freemasonry, which was part of that religion.

In this sense, the Anglican clergyman Anderson said that Freemasonry is the "ancient" religion with which all people agree. He was not referring to some foreign pagan religion, but the original biblical religion revealed at the dawn of history.

Biblical Origins

Anderson, Hutchinson, Oliver and the other early writers did not claim that Buddha was the first Mason as Pike did, but referred to the following biblical characters as being the first members of the Craft.

- Adam The Patriarchs
- Cain Joseph
- Abel Moses

- Seth Solomon and the builders of the Temple
- Lamech and sons John the Baptist
- Tubal-Cain Jesus
- Nimrod St. John and St. Andrew
- Noah and his sons King Herod
- The builders of the tower of Babel

Some early writers also traced the origin of Freemasonry to John the Baptist, the beginning of the Christian church when the ancient true religion restored. Others refereed to the Crusades or to certain pre-Reformation movements which sought to return to the pure Christian faith.

Criticisms

The attempt to find the origins of Freemasonry in a prebiblical religion or in the Bible is an exercise in futility. There is absolutely nothing in the Bible about Freemasonry. To say that Adam's fig leaf was a Masonic apron stretches all credulity. Masons have traditionally been told that the Craft began with the building of Solomon's Temple. But there is nothing in the biblical record that even remotely hints at this idea.

Masons have also been told that the legend of Hiram Abiff, which plays an important role in the third degree, is a part of the biblical record. But, in truth, the legend of Hiram Abiff has nothing to do with the Bible.

The legend is nowhere recorded in Scripture. We are not told where, how, or by whom Hiram died. As a matter of fact, the

Masonic legend combines several different individuals in the Bible called Hiram or Hirum into one composite individual. The legend has no basis in fact.

Conclusion

While we cannot accept these early theories of where Masonry began, it does reveal that for nearly two centuries, the Craft was viewed as a Christian institution completely compatible with biblical religion. The idea that Freemasonry came from pagan origins never crossed its early members' minds.

Author's Note: This article was adapted from "The Truth about Masons" by Robert Morey. Harvest House Publishers, Copyright ©1993 ISBN -56507-077-1: Chapter 2

CHAPTER 2
Our Hidden Masonic Resource

Brethren, their appetites satisfied with the meal they just shared, filed into the auditorium with great anticipation of what was to come. It was one of many area meetings held by MWB Gail Turner. This one just happened to be in St. Joseph, MO. The brethren received more than they had anticipated. Most expected the usual introduction of themes and reports. However, what they got fed; was food not for the stomach but for the mind. This area meeting contained meat. The kind of meat that one chews, digests, and reflects upon. The theme of "Connectivity," having been introduced, began to be elaborated on by the various officers. Then RWB Jon Broyles, our Junior Grand Warden, discussed our Hidden Masonic Resource.

The phrase "You can't see the forest for the trees" came to mind as RWB Broyles talked about part of this resource we have in our fraternity. We have officers who were given charge over a cache of hidden wealth and have a tendency to administer its care by the letter of the law. Some of these officers dispense their authority over this hidden asset with great care, like a grandmother keeping the recipe for her famous cookies as a dark secret hidden from everyone. Some widely distribute the coins of knowledge from our Hidden Masonic Resource to all who need their "wages paid them in part at least in those valuable instructions therein received."

Our hidden Masonic resource is what separates us from other fraternal and social organizations. It is what helps us to make good men better.

It is what allows men to grow into dynamic individuals and develop the leadership skills required for sitting in the East and become the leaders that are hidden within all of us. It is the foundation or the ground floor of our fraternity. We call it, are you ready for this, some even shudder at its name, RITUAL. Oh, my word. There I said it. Ritual.

Yes, our Ritual is the Hidden Masonic Resource visible to all, learned by most, and ignored by some. A lot of brethren has missed the meanings contained within our Ritual. Why are these lessons missed? Where can we learn them, and especially, why are they important to us as Masons?

Let us examine these issues one at a time. First, our forefathers and the generations that preceded us were learned men. They learned the Ritual by word of mouth.

This learning was reinforced by what was read in the Great Light, by the sermons preached in their churches and by common sense. Then the book titled "King Solomon and His Followers" appeared on the scene. The King Solomon was one of the first cipher books published. It was published by an independent publisher and had errors but was generally accurate for each grand lodge's Ritual. Its use was forbidden in most Grand Lodges because, at that time, having the Ritual in written form was not allowed; however, most, not all, the brethren used this book to learn their proficiencies, parts of degrees, and the lectures (I must confess that when I was learning my work in the early Seventies that book was invaluable because I could read it when my instructor and coach was not around). What was missed? What did I miss in my early learning? The Ritual started to become words to be recited.

Its execution was to be word perfect, and this still is the greatest care we emphasize in our ritual learning. We missed the knowledge of those that came before us. We missed the reason that the Ritual was written as it was in its beginning.

In the Dark Ages, preachers and teachers of religious thought and doctrine used common symbols and tools to illustrate the points Scripture taught. Since most craftsmen and people of that time period couldn't read or write, relating the lessons to the everyday items they saw and used helped them to remember what was taught on a daily basis. Our Ritual was developed over time, and the early versions of our Ritual used the implements of operative Masons as examples of what lesson was to be taught by a certain portion of the ceremony. This practice still continues today by most preachers. They still use illustrations and examples to drive home the point they are trying to make. We can learn the foundation of the teachings of our fraternity by adapting the virtues taught by the Ritual.

I recently attended a session sponsored by the Scottish Rite in which the Sovereign Grand Inspector General of Tennessee, Illustrious Brother Hoyt Samples spoke. He did a presentation on "connecting" with the younger Masons through Masonic Education and Mentoring. His observations indicated that when the younger brethren listen to discussions of the minutes of the previous meeting and what type of beans are going to fixed for the next meal, they leave unfulfilled in Masonic knowledge and don't return. His research indicated that the younger generation coming into our lodges and the Scottish Rite are starved for and are seeking knowledge.

I have seen this in my own district time after time. At regular meetings that I attend, the younger masons come to ask me questions about the Ritual. These questions are not centered on the execution of it but upon why we do it this way or that way. They ask about the meaning of a certain portion or where it applies in their lives.

Like Ill. Br. Samples has alluded to, these Masons "want for proper education and knowledge." So, who has the responsibility for instructing these brethren? We do.

All of us. Not only the District Deputy Grand Lecturers, Regional Grand Lecturers, the Grand Lecturer, but every one of us has the duty and responsibility of teaching the younger Masons. Our Grand Lodge, the Scottish Rite, and other Masonic organizations have named it the Mentoring Program. Not only does a Mentoring program allow a newly made Mason a method by which to learn, but its importance will be measured by those who pass the knowledge on to future generations. Let me quote from the Entered Apprentice Charge, "At your leisure hours that you may improve in Masonic knowledge you are to converse with well-informed Brethren who will be always ready to give, as you will be to receive, instruction."[4] Brethren, this is, in essence, the Masonic Education and Mentoring Programs. We all received this charge to begin its implementation when we entered Masonry. We have heard it many times over our

---

[4] The Masonic Manual of the Grand Lodge A.F. and A.M. of Missouri, the Grand Lodge 1952, page 41.

careers as Masons, but have we really heard what it said? This sentence was not put into the charge to give the author a higher word count.

It was put in there to charge us all to become knowledgeable in Masonic lessons. To impart that knowledge to the younger Masons entering the fraternity is a duty not to be taken lightly.

We have, at our grasp, the opportunity of a lifetime. It's called influencing the life of a brother. And as such, by virtue of command in the EA charge, we must "practice what we preach." That, my brothers, is the heart of the Mentoring Program and the Masonic Education Program of this Grand Lodge. Practicing what we preach. I will confess and admit that I have failed at this. As a District Lecturer, I have failed to teach the Ritual's lessons while teaching its execution, and I am most sincerely sorry for my short-sightedness. In some of my recent schools, I have received a better response when I teach the how's and why's and lessons of certain portions of a part we are working on.

Since implementing these changes, attendance has increased and shows that the Masonic Education and Mentoring programs work well.

As you learn the Ritual to fulfill an office, learn the meaning behind the words. Will you strive to understand the why of an expression and pass that knowledge on? The survival of keeping our younger Masons in the fraternity may depend significantly on whether or not we pass on the lessons contained within the greatest Masonic resource we have – the Ritual.

CHAPTER 3

MASONIC CHARITY

Chris sat, with two friends, in the picture window of a quaint restaurant just off the corner of the town square in a small Missouri town called Weston. Chris had just cleaned and spruced up the lodge for the upcoming official visit of the District Master. The food and the company, locals from the community, were both especially good that day.

As they talked, his attention was drawn outside, across the street. There, walking into town, was a man who appeared to be carrying all his worldly goods on his back. He was holding a well-worn sign that read, 'I will work for food.' Chris' heart sank. He was the one who helped to organize the annual Christmas outreach to the needy in the community, and he brought him to the attention of his friends and noticed that others around us had stopped eating to focus on him.

Heads moved in a mixture of sadness and disbelief.

They continued with their meal, but his image lingered in his mind. They finished the meal and went their separate ways. Everyone had errands, and Chris was no exception and quickly set out to accomplish them. He glanced toward the town square, looking somewhat halfheartedly for the strange visitor. He was fearful, knowing that seeing him again would call some response, and drove through town and saw nothing of him. He made some purchases at a store and got back in his car.

Chris thought about the master's charge in the first degree, "…this demand was not made in the spirit of levity, but to teach you a lesson in Charity, which next to a belief in Deity lies and the foundation of Freemasonry. "Deep within him, the Spirit of God kept speaking to Chris: 'Don't go back to the office until you've at least driven once more around the square.' Then with some hesitancy, he headed back into town. He saw him as he turned the square's third corner standing on the steps of the church, going through his sack. He stopped and looked; feeling both compelled to speak to him yet wanting to drive on. The empty parking space on the corner seemed to be a sign from God: an invitation to park he pulled in, got out and approached the town's newest visitor.

'Looking for the pastor?' He asked.

'Not really,' he replied, 'just resting.'

'Have you eaten today?'

'Oh, I ate something early this morning.'

'Would you like to have lunch with me?' Chris asked.

'Do you have some work I could do for you?'

'No work,' he replied. 'I commute here to work from the city, but I would like to take you to lunch.'

'Sure,' he replied with a smile.

As he began to gather his things, Chris asked some surface questions. Where you headed?'

St. Louis.'

'Where you from?'

'Oh, all over; mostly Florida.'

'How long you been walking?'

'Fourteen years,' came the reply.

He knew he had met someone unusual. They sat across from each other in the same restaurant Chris had left earlier. The stranger's face was weathered slightly beyond his 38 years. His eyes were dark yet clear, and he spoke with startling eloquence and articulation. He removed his jacket to reveal a bright red T-shirt that said, 'Jesus is The Never-Ending Story.'

Then Daniel's story began to unfold. He had seen rough times early in life. He'd made some wrong choices and reaped the consequences. Fourteen years earlier, he had stopped on the beach in Daytona while backpacking across the country. He tried to hire on with some men who were putting up a large tent and some equipment. A concert, he thought.

He was hired, but the tent would not house a concert but revival services, and in those services, he saw life more clearly. So he gave his life over to God. 'Nothing's been the same since,' he said, 'I felt the Lord telling me to keep walking, and so I did, some 14 years now.' 'Ever think of stopping?' Chris asked.

'Oh, once in a while, when it seems to get the best of me, but God has given me this calling. I give out Bibles that's what's in my sack. I work to buy food and Bibles, and I give them out when His Spirit leads.'

Chris was amazed. The new homeless friend was not homeless. He was on a mission and lived this way by choice. The question burned inside for a moment and then he finally asked: 'What's it like?

"What?"

'To walk into a town carrying all your things on your back and to show your sign?'

'Oh, it was humiliating at first. People would stare and make comments. Once someone tossed a piece of half-eaten bread and made a gesture that certainly didn't make me feel welcome. But then it became humbling to realize that God was using me to touch lives and change people's concepts of other folks like me.'

Chris' concept was changing, too. They finished the dessert and gathered Daniel's things. Just outside the door, he paused and turned to Chris and said, 'Come Ye blessed of my Father and inherit the kingdom I've prepared for you. For when I was hungry you gave me food, when I was thirsty you gave me drink, a stranger and you took me in.' Chris felt as if he were on holy ground. Chris then asked, "Could you use another Bible?"

Daniel said he preferred a certain translation. It traveled well and was not too heavy. It was also his personal favorite. 'I've read through it 14 times,' he said.

'I'm not sure we've got one of those, but let's stop by our church and see' Chris was able to find his new friend a Bible that would do well, and he seemed very grateful. 'Where are you headed from here?' he asked.

'Well, I found this little map on the back of this amusement park coupon.'

'Are you hoping to hire on there for a while?'

'No, I just figure I should go there. I figure someone under that star right there needs a Bible, so that's where I'm going next.'

He smiled, and the warmth of his spirit radiated the sincerity of his mission. He drove him back to the town-square where they had met two hours earlier, and as they drove, it started raining. Chris parked and helped Daniel unload his things.

'Would you sign my autograph book?' Daniel asked. 'I like to keep messages from folks I meet.'

Chris wrote in his little book that his commitment to his calling had touched his life. I encouraged him to stay strong. And he left him with a verse of scripture from Jeremiah, 'I know the plans I have for you, declared the Lord, 'plans to prosper you and not to harm you; Plans to give you a future and a hope.'[5]

'Thanks, man,' he said. 'I know we just met and we're really just strangers, but I love you.'

'I know,' Chris said, 'I love you, too.' 'The Lord is good!'

'Yes, He is. How long has it been since someone hugged you?' Chris asked.

A long time,' he replied.

---

[5] Jeremiah 29:11, The Holy Bible, New International Version, Copyright 1973, 1978, 1984 International Bible Society. Used by permission of Zondervan Bible Publishers.

And so, on the busy street corner in the drizzling rain, the new friends embraced, and Chris felt deep inside that he had been changed. A feeling he had not had since being raised a Master Mason. Daniel put his things on his back, smiled his winning smile and said, 'See you in the New Jerusalem.'

'I'll be there!' was Chris' reply.

Daniel began his journey again. He headed away with his sign dangling from his bedroll and pack of Bibles. He stopped, turned and said, 'When you see something that makes you think of me, will you pray for me? "You bet,' Chris shouted back, 'God bless.'

'God bless.' And that was the last he saw of him.

Late that evening as he left his office, the wind blew strong. The cold front had settled hard upon the town. He bundled up and hurried to the car. As he sat back and reached for the emergency brake, he saw them, a pair of well-worn brown work gloves neatly laid over the length of the handle. He picked them up and thought of his new friend and wondered if his hands would stay warm that night without them.

It was then he remembered his words: 'If you see something that makes you think of me; will you pray for me?'

Today his gloves lie on Chris' desk in his office for all to see. They help him to see the world and its people in a new way, and they help him remember those two hours with his unique friend and to pray for his ministry. 'See you in the New Jerusalem,' he said. Yes, Daniel, I know I will...

Masonic charity has a twofold effect as demonstrated by the interaction of Chris and Daniel and represented in Chris' life by a pair of worn work gloves. Moved by his desire to help, Chris entertained Daniel through a small lunch. Daniel, relating his personal story to Chris, Chris found himself changed in ways he had not felt in a long time. Inner commitments that had diminished over time and inner beliefs that were once buried were brought alive by a simple act of providing a little lunch someone had called Masonic Charity.

Masonic charity knows no size or bounds. It may be as grandiose as organizing a massive outreach and raising thousands or as simple as giving relief to one stranger in a small-town restaurant. It may be a campaign to support some worthy cause or just giving a dollar to support a child's effort to help fund the baseball team.

Masonic charity starts and ends within our own hearts. Some give as they know they will be recognized, and they have their reward. However, often times it is the smallest act of charity that has the biggest reward. It is not the amount or the publicity, for I doubt that anyone hardly noticed what Chris did for Daniel, but the touching of one soul to another in gratitude. It is the small acts of kindness that change both parties, so they grow and feel fulfilled in ways known only to them. A Mason's search for knowledge and the meaning of Masonry starts with one small act of kindness.

Masonry defines Charity as the inward and outward acts of love. The Apostle Paul evaluated the three essential virtues of the Christian religion as Faith, Hope and Charity. Masonry places charity at the topmost rung of its mystic ladder because of the importance of the virtue. It should, like the cornerstone of a building, be the foundation upon which a Mason starts his Masonic knowledge and character building. We have learned in 1 Cor 8: 1b that knowledge puffs up the ego of an individual but Love (Charity) builds the character. Charity is the cementing bond of Masonry.

When compared to the Christian doctrine of Charity, it is evident that both show that Charity is broader, longer, deeper, and higher than any other type of aid to the poor and destitute. It includes help of any sort but is fueled by love. We need only to look at the love chapter as found in 1 Cor 13: 1-13. Even as Paul describes Love in this passage of Scripture, Masonic Charity reaches the same depth of love.

We have seen two foundations of Masonry at work in our story. The first is Charity but the deeper lesson learned by Chris was that of Love. Not the kind of love a man has for his wife and family, but the true definition of Brotherly Love. It sometimes is easier to teach men to love through Charity as the basis of building successful bonds with other men than any other type of learning. By the simple act of charity, the Mason not only learns about how love can manifest itself, but he can begin to see the path he must start down. If he searches this lesson in the Bible, he will find that Jesus' entire ministry was established and rooted in love and manifested by the charitable acts of healing and other miracles he performed.

The life and ministry of Jesus is the best and most complete example of Charity that the Mason can emulate. Christ demonstrated the ultimate charitable act by sacrificing himself on the Cross so that we may live. Masonically, the symbolic emblem most associated with this particular act is the ever green, ever living Sprig of Faith which blooms at the head of the Grave. This can be symbolized by the Sprig of Acacia or an Evergreen sprig. It is set there to remind him of the immortality that can possibly be his should he choose to accept Christ as his savior.

Some lodges, like Daniel in our story, hand new candidates a copy of the Bible. Among its vast contents are the answers to the simple questions each degree presents to the Mason. It also can contain the deeper meanings to the more serious questions and start the Mason on a quest which has no end.

I am reminded of another story which demonstrates what Love manifested by Charity can do and the effects it can have on other people.

While Mrs. Miller was bagging some early potatoes for me, I noticed a small boy, delicate of bone and feature, ragged but clean, hungrily appraising a basket of freshly picked green peas. I paid for my potatoes but was also drawn to the display of fresh green peas. I am a pushover for creamed peas and new potatoes. Pondering the peas, I couldn't help overhearing the conversation between Mr. Miller and the ragged boy next to me.

"Hello Barry, how are you today?"

"H'lo, Mr. Miller. Fine, thank ya. Jus' admirin' them peas. sure look good."

"They are good, Barry. How's your Ma?"

"Fine. Gittin' stronger alla' time."

"Good. Anything I can help you with?"

"No, Sir. Jus' admirin' them peas."

"Would you like to take some home?"

"No, Sir. Got nuthin' to pay for 'em with."

"Well, what have you to trade me for some of those peas?"

"All I got's my prize marble here."

"Is that right? Let me see it."

"Here 'tis. She's a dandy."

"I can see that. Hmmmmm, only thing is this one is blue and I sort of go for red. Do you have a red one like this at home?"

"Not zackley. But almost."

"Tell you what. Take this sack of peas home with you and next trip this way let me look at that red marble."

"Sure will. Thanks Mr. Miller."

Mrs. Miller, who had been standing nearby, came over to help me. With a smile she said, "There are two other boys like him in our community, all three are in very poor circumstances. Jim just loves to bargain with them for peas, apples, tomatoes, or whatever. When they come back with their red marbles, and they always do, he decides he doesn't like red after all and he sends them home with a bag of produce for a green marble or an orange one, perhaps."

I left the stand smiling to myself, impressed with this man. A short time later I moved to Colorado, but I never forgot the story of this man, the boys, and their bartering.

Several years went by, each more rapid that the previous one. Just recently I had occasion to visit some old friends in that Idaho community and while I was there learned that Mr. Miller had died. They were having his viewing that evening and knowing my friends wanted to go, I agreed to accompany them. Upon arrival at the mortuary we fell into line to meet the relatives of the deceased and to offer whatever words of comfort we could.

Ahead of us in line were three young men. One was in an army uniform and the other two wore nice haircuts, dark suits and white shirts ... all very professional looking.

They approached Mrs. Miller, standing composed and smiling by her husband's casket. Each of the young men hugged her, kissed her on the cheek, spoke briefly with her and moved on to the casket.

Her misty light blue eyes followed them as, one by one, each young man stopped briefly and placed his own warm hand over the cold pale hand in the casket. Each left the mortuary awkwardly, wiping his eyes.

Our turn came to meet Mrs. Miller. I told her who I was and mentioned the story she had told me about the marbles. With her eyes glistening, she took my hand and led me to the casket.

"Those three young men who just left were the boys I told you about. They just told me how they appreciated the things Jim "traded" them. Now, at last, when Jim could not change his mind about color or size ... they came to pay their debt."

"We've never had a great deal of the wealth of this world," she confided, "but right now, Jim would consider himself the richest man in Idaho."

With loving gentleness, she lifted the lifeless fingers of her deceased husband. Resting underneath were three exquisitely shined red marbles.[6]

In the Fifty-Year presentation from the Grand Lodge of Missouri, there is a paragraph which emphasizes charity. One of those sentences reads, "… through its various lodges, given relief to the indigent, charity to the widow, and guidance to the orphan." This confirmation of our core charity belief has been in Missouri's ceremonies since it was written and published when MWB William R. Denslow was Grand Master of Missouri in 1967. However, those affirmations have been in our ceremonies and degree obligations since the inception of the Grand Lodges in the United States. So, how old are those instructions?

We find in the Old Testament these words from Exodus chapter 22 verse 22, "Do not take advantage of a widow or an orphan." Again, and again, our Bible has instruction for us from the Father. We find those instructions in Deuteronomy chapter 24 verses 19 through 21 "When you are harvesting in your field and you overlook a sheaf, do not go back to get it. Leave it for the alien, the fatherless and the widow, so that the LORD your God may bless you in all the work of your hands. When you beat the olives from your trees, do not go over the branches a second time. Leave what remains for the alien, the

---

[6] Petersen, W.E., "Three Red Marbles, Ensign Magazine, October, 1975, p.39. Church of Jesus Christ of Latter-Day Saints.

fatherless and the widow. When you harvest the grapes in your vineyard, do not go over the vines again. Leave what remains for the alien, the fatherless and the widow".

One very special command comes from Deuteronomy 26:12 which reads, "When you have finished setting aside a tenth of all your produce in the third year, the year of the tithe, you shall give it to the Levite, the alien, the fatherless and the widow, so that they may eat in your towns and be satisfied." What a reminder of the obligation we voluntarily place ourselves under when we kneel at the altar.

Weston Lodge # 53 in Weston, Missouri, has been showing us an example of how to keep this obligation in the local community. Every year the lodge sells fresh fruit by the case to the community as a fund raiser for its Christmas Charity Program. Each year the fruit arrives and on the Saturday before Christmas, the lodge and various members of the community, make up over 400 fruit trays, 20 completed meal boxes for families in need, and the same number in gift bags for the children. It could be these verses in the Old Testament along with the verses in the New Testament which inspired the Biblical basis for the creation of our various charities.

Through the light of these verses we may, like our forefathers before us, allow them to be the guiding Scriptural foundations for other areas in your life not only as Masons but as members of the Human race.

Remember the moral of the story is that we will not be remembered by our words, but by our kind deeds.

As a Mason, you stood before the Master divested of all metallic substances, neither naked or clothed, neither barefoot or with shoes and was asked for some metallic substance, that it might be laid up in the archives as a memorial that you had been made a Mason. But what was that really teaching you? It was teaching you the lesson of charity. Not only with a member of the fraternity but with the entire Human Family. Some grand lodge jurisdictions drive this lesson home in a dramatic way, when you could not comply with the demand a brother came to your relief. A lesson which would not be easily forgotten.

Let me end this by asking a simple question. Will you barter your love of mankind, kindness, and charity for a Red Marble and place a pair of gloves on your desk as a reminder to contribute and pray for those in need?

CHAPTER 4

THE PLUMB LINE

In our Masonic careers we are taught that the plumb Line teaches moral rectitude and walking upright before God and man. But where did the teaching originate?

When you first entered a lodge of Fellow Crafts you heard these words of Scripture found in Amos 7 verses 7-9 which read:

"This is what he showed me: The Lord was standing by a wall that had been built true to plumb, with a plumb line in his hand. And the LORD asked me, "What do you see, Amos?"

"A plumb line," I replied.

Then the Lord said, "Look, I am setting a plumb line among my people Israel; I will spare them no longer." (NIV) The King James Version and the New King James version uses the phrase "I will not pass by them anymore." The Jewish Neviim, (prophetic writings) of Scripture uses the word "over" in place of the word "pass" as found in the KJV and the NKJV.

If we take a look at the verses the Grand Lodge of Missouri chose for the ritual, we find in verse 7 that the Lord was standing by the wall that had been built by a plumb line. Operative Masons still use the plumb to check verticals, raise columns and other uses. Since God had the plumb line in his hand, we know that the wall was built true and plumb. The King James Version says that the Lord stood UPON a wall made by a plumb line. What is not clarified in Amos' vision and prophecy is what was it a wall of or to. Was it a wall of the New Jerusalem? Was it a wall of the existing Jerusalem? Was it the wall of the Temple or just a wall in the middle of Space?

Either way what does that wall represent to you?

Notice again in the verse that the Lord is standing by or on the wall. I submit to you that Masonically speaking, the Great Architect of the Universe is watching how you build your moral and Masonic edifice.

As we look at verse 8, notice that God asks Amos what he sees. His answer is very important. Amos replies that he sees a plumb line. Do you think that it was the traditional plumb line? Some scholars have suggested, and rightly so, that the object lesson here is that Israel needed to be checked spiritually as well as morally with the laws handed down by Moses. Amos' prophecy was not only a rebuke and declaration of judgment from moving away from faith and obedience to the Lord but a warning of the coming destruction of Israel and especially to Jerusalem.

Other scholars, especially those who study all the prophets of Israel, agree that the prophecies of the writing prophets are in agreement when it comes to the messianic prophecy. With this in mind, do you think that Amos saw something different other than a literal plumb line?

The Lord tells Amos that he will set a plumb line in the midst or among His people Israel. Notice the descriptive noun Amos uses. Midst or Among. The scholars of today and yesterday, as published in most commentaries on this prophet, say the Lord is setting a literal guide among the people for their spiritual growth and measurement to the Lords will for Israel. If that is the case, it would allude to the Lord sending another prophet to speak to Israel with the same authority and recognition as those that have come before. In the last half of verse 9 God says that He will not pass by or spare them anymore. God either dwelt with or through the prophets of Israel most all the time until the messianic era. Yes, there were vast spans of time between prophets and occurrences, but He still kept his word and watchful care over Israel directly. Notice that God says He will not pass by or spare them anymore. If that is so, then to what does the plumb line or to whom does it refer?

We may get a hint of the meaning of that plumb line in the third degree. The second half of that degree alludes to the "Lion of the Tribe of Judah" in a prayer. Is there a possibility that maybe, just maybe, that sign post might be telling us who that plumb line is and where we should be looking for the answer? Could it be that Amos was telling us that the Lord himself will be watching us build the walls of our Masonic edifice with a plumb line. A plumb line of Brotherly Love, Relief, and Truth?

I leave that for you to personally answer according to your own faith and beliefs.

CHAPTER 5
THE WOODEN BOWL

I attended a Lodge meeting in my district not long ago and watched with curiosity as to how the members treated an old past master as he joined the fellowship meal before the meeting. They were not intentionally rude or derogatory toward the aging past master but still the incident pondered the question as to how we treat the old timers who attend our meetings. What begged the question was that he sat alone not only at the meal but in the Lodge meeting also.

Very few came to inquire as to how he was doing or say a word to him. No one sat with him; I am guilty as well because I did not sit with him either in the meeting. Yes, I feel guilty of the same style of attitude and behavior. On the way home I got to thinking about the meeting when my guilt took over and I had to have a conversation with Grand Architect of the Universe for my actions. It was during this conversation with God that and old story about a Wooden Bowl came to me as an illustration of life.

A frail old man went to live with his son, daughter-in-law, and four-year-old grandson. The old man's hands trembled, his eyesight was blurred, and his step faltered.

The family ate together at the table. But the elderly grandfather's shaky hands and failing sight made eating difficult. Peas rolled off his spoon onto the floor. When he grasped the glass, milk spilled on the tablecloth. The son and daughter-in-law became irritated with the mess.

'We must do something about father,' said the son. 'I've had enough of his spilled milk, noisy eating, and food on the floor.' So the husband and wife set a small table in the corner. There, Grandfather ate alone while the rest of the family enjoyed dinner.

Since Grandfather had broken a dish or two, his food was served in a wooden bowl. When the family glanced in Grandfather's direction, sometimes he had a tear in his eye as he sat alone. Still, the only words the couple had for him were sharp admonitions when he dropped a fork or spilled food.

The four-year-old watched it all in silence. One evening before supper, the father noticed his son playing with wood scraps on the floor.

He asked the child sweetly, 'What are you making?'

Just as sweetly, the boy responded, 'Oh, I am making a little bowl for you and Mama to eat your food in when I grow up.' The four-year-old smiled and went back to work.

The words so struck the parents that they were speechless. Then tears started to stream down their cheeks. Though no word was spoken, both knew what must be done.

That evening the husband took Grandfather's hand and gently led him back to the family table. For the remainder of his days he ate every meal with the family. And for some reason, neither husband nor wife seemed to care any longer when a fork was dropped, milk spilled, or the tablecloth soiled. (Adapted from "The Old Man and

His Grandson"; Tale # 78; Grimm's Fairy Tales; The Brothers Grimm)

It was then revealed what an allusion to our motto, "Making Good Men Better," could represent. In support of this I am reminded of the incident in the Old Testament of Scripture where Israel asked God what they should do to walk with Him. God's answer is found in Micah 6:8, "He has shown you, O man, what is good and what does the Lord require of you? To act justly, and to love mercy, and to walk humbly with your God."

God had told them this once before in Deuteronomy 10:12, when God, through the author of Deuteronomy, prophesied "And now, O Israel, what does the Lord your God ask of you but to fear the Lord your God, to walk in all his ways, to love him, to serve the Lord your God with all your heart and with all your soul, and to observe the Lord's commands and decrees that I am giving you today for your own good."

I find it interesting to see how the Tenants and four Cardinal Virtues of our institution are incorporated and revealed in these two verses of the Great Light of Masonry, especially Brotherly Love.

Did the old past master feel like the grandfather in the story? Did he have a tear in his eye while he was eating and attending the meeting? Was his heart broken by the lack of Brotherly Love shown to him during his visit? More importantly, will he return and impart to the younger members some of the Masonic wisdom his age group possesses?

Masonic wisdom does not always come from the ritual of our great fraternity. It comes from the application of the knowledge acquired through it and applied to our own lives. The older generation of Masons possesses such a vast knowledge of wisdom that we often-times overlook them for guidance and instruction. Not only does their knowledge explain some of the history of our local Lodges, but it is also the application of their personal experiences that have greatest value.

Our younger Masons have yet to learn the old adage, "The older I get the smarter my parents get." This can be applied to masonry as well by changing the word parents to Old Timers. We have a tendency, by nature of our creation, to associate with those most like us and our age. Yet, why do some cultures live with and support their parents and grandparents in the same household for generations? They were taught at a very early age what these verses of the Holy Writings meant whether they were of our faith or not.

They learned that wisdom for life can come from the parents and grandparents. They learned respect for that wisdom and respect for them as individuals as well. This is something we take for granted and put on the back shelf a lot. I know I am really guilty of this. But knowledge coupled with application equals wisdom. So, if we bring them back with us at mealtime and let them eat off of the same plates we use, will we be better men for the experience?

I don't know. But I do know this: all of my experiences have shown that a warm heart towards our older Brethren, our elderly parents, others of that age will bring untold amounts of joy which has no comparison.

We have been taught the duties of walking with our God and the definitions of Brotherly Love but how many times have you heard about the rewards? Very few I would assume. Remember the pomegranate in the second-degree lecture? It represents plenty. The amount of Brotherly Love and relief given will have an impact on the number of seeds of joy in your pomegranate.

What have we learned through our examples? Our conclusion comes from the wise words of Dr. Maya Angelou:

"I know that I've learned life sometimes gives you a second chance. I've learned that you shouldn't go through life with a catcher's mitt on both hands. You need to be able to throw something back sometimes. I've learned that if you pursue happiness, it will elude you."

But, if you focus on your family, your friends, the needs of others, your work and doing the very best you can, happiness will find you. I've learned that whenever you decide something with an open heart, you will usually make the right decision. I've learned that even when I have pains, I don't have to be one. I've learned that every day, you and I should reach out and touch someone.

People love that human touch — holding hands, a warm hug, or just a friendly pat on the back. I've learned that I still have a lot to learn.

CHAPTER 6

SUBDUE THE PASSIONS

During the opening of a lodge of Entered Apprentices the following question, in one form or another, is asked: "What come you here to do?" The answer from that officer contains the phrase, "to learn to subdue my passions."

Passion, in today's dictionaries, is defined as any powerful emotion or appetite such as love, joy, hatred, anger or greed. An ardent adoring desire such as lust and an abandoned display of emotion especially anger. Biblically, the word passion refers to evil desires or as some would call them the sinful nature. Romans 7:5 says, "For when we were controlled by the sinful nature, the sinful passions aroused by the law were at work in our bodies, so that we bore fruit for death." Titus 2:12 states, "It teaches us to say "No" to ungodliness and worldly passions, and to live self-controlled, upright and godly lives in this present age…" We also find in Galatians 5:24 and 25 the following, "Those who belong to Christ Jesus have crucified the sinful nature with its passions and desires. Since we live by the Spirit, let us keep in step with the Spirit. Let us not become conceited, provoking and envying each other."

When we combine subdue, which means to conquer or vanquish; or to quiet or bring under control, the lesson of this statement starts to enlighten the Mason as to a character quality and a behavior consistent with his religion. Masonically, everyone enters the fraternity on the same level. We are all received in the same manner and taught the same lessons. It is what we do with those lessons that make the difference. As with any organization, whether it is a church, fraternity, or civic group, passions start to develop. Political goals and ambitions within an organization can be its undoing. Growing up I remember the Soviet Union Premier, Nakita Kruchev making the statement that they would bury us within our own borders. He was referring to the youth and the school systems. Not only is this important to the wellbeing of the fraternity but it has a greater meaning in our personal lives. One of the Masonic philosophies is "Making Good Men Better." This lesson of subduing the passions applies to this area of a Mason's life.

Titus 2:12 teaches a Mason to say "No" to ungodliness and worldly passions, and to live self-controlled, upright, and godly lives in this present age. As we learn in the Book of James our actions speak louder than our words. Obi Wan Kenobi told Anikin Skywalker, "be mindful of your thoughts; they betray you." Our actions are a direct reflection of our thoughts. Our actions can also influence our thoughts. As Masons we conduct ourselves in a manner which should be reflected throughout the community and our families. If these actions are a reflection of what we are taught, then it behooves the Mason to learn a different thought pattern and behavioral action.

Those behavioral actions and thought patterns are the other side of subduing our passions called self-control. Keeping peace and harmony in a lodge is paramount. I remember a certain lodge meeting in which the members were discussing the need to donate a commercial disposal to the kitchen of a middle school. This middle school allowed the lodge to host several fund-raising dinners by which they made their contributory budget and donate a portion back to the school. The debate as to whether the lodge could spend the couple of thousand dollars to get the disposal was intense to say the least. Having several thousand dollars in the savings account, the affordability was not the issue. The issue extended deeper. A belief was held by a couple of older members who would not consent to let the balance fall below a certain level. This belief caused hurt feelings and discord among the brethren. My point here is that had the brethren used self-control, the confrontation would have been a discussion and would have had a different effect. Proverbs 25:28 says, "Like a city whose walls are broken down is a man who lacks self-control."

Whether we are involved in our church setting, fraternal setting or with our family, the ability to exercise self-control builds healthy relationships. In 2 Peter 1:5 – 8 we learn, For this very reason, make every effort to add to your faith goodness; and to goodness, knowledge; and to knowledge, self-control; and to self-control, perseverance; and to perseverance, godliness; and to godliness, brotherly kindness; and to brotherly kindness, love. For if you possess these qualities in increasing measure, they will keep you from being ineffective and unproductive in your knowledge of our Lord Jesus Christ." As our faith growths in Christ our character qualities change because of our desire to emulate Christ and what he taught us. It is no different for the Mason. His interaction with members of other religions and different walks of life allows him the opportunity to display the Godly characteristics of Christ through the words he says and the actions he takes.

This question in the opening ritual is designed to remind him of this obligation he has to his fellow man. With the altar setting in the middle of the lodge room and the Holy Bible resting open upon it, the words of this question should nudge him to seek the Great Light for instruction in this sublime principle. 1 Corinthians 9:25 (KJV) "And every man that striveth for the mastery is temperate (Self Controlled) in all things. Now they do it to obtain a corruptible crown; but we an incorruptible." The NIV says it this way, "Everyone who competes in the games goes into strict training. They do it to get a crown that will not last; but we do it to get a crown that will last forever." Notice that the NIV uses the term "competes in the games".

Are we not competing in the game of life and with ourselves to become the best Christ has called us to be? Masonry's ritual is replete with lessons pointing to the attributes of Godly living. In competing in the game of life, we as Christians have but one goal and that is to lead others to Christ. The character quality of being self-controlled or subduing the passions is only one of the character qualities Christ displayed in his life here on earth. If we as Masons are to live up to our calling as Christians, we should endeavor to incorporate this principle into our daily lives; by doing so we will become what Christ referred to as the Salt of the Earth. From a Masonic perspective, we do not have or teach any specific religion, however, by displaying the qualities in our ritualistic lessons we take on the attributes and attitudes of Christ thereby drawing others to us. This drawing others allows us to meet with a brother at an appropriate time and share with him our particular faith.

Since being self-controlled is a leadership quality also, we find that people will seek us out for council and advice. This puts a great responsibility on the Mason in the fact that his advice not only has to be Godly in its content but also Masonically correct.

So the question is this, are we willing as Masons, to adhere to what the ritual is teaching through the Great Light of Masonry by the Great Creator of the Universe? Are we willing to put into action those principles of behavior and actions to display those qualities which are so essential to being a good mason or are we going to leave those lessons closed up in the Great Light and only read them when we have a part to say?

I beseech you, my brethren, that due consideration is to your benefit as well as to the benefit of the others within your charge as masons. Some of us are officers and others have served a time with patience but are still imparting those lessons we have or are continuing to learn. I urge you to consider what you have read and put into action what you have learned so that you, my brother, can be and example of the phrase, "Making Good Men Better."

CHAPTER 7

JUSTICE AND JUDGEMENT

Proverbs 21:3 says; "To do justice and judgment is more acceptable to the Lord than sacrifice."

Our desire for justice for ourselves and for others often complicates the issues, builds up factions and quarrels. Worldly justice and unworldly justice are quite different things. The supernatural approach, when understood, is to turn the other cheek, to give up what one has, willingly, gladly, with no spirit of martyrdom, to rejoice in being the least, to being unrecognized, the slightest. (Dorothy Day, "Reflections," Christianity Today, Vol. 44, no. 10. See: Matthew 5:39; Matthew 20:24-28; Philippians 2:1-8).

One of the main lessons of the of the 3rd Degree, according to the volume of the Sacred Law as found in Matthew 7:1, is to reinforce the lesson contained within the Entered Apprentice degree and teach us to act uprightly in our dealings with all mankind, and never fail to act justly toward ourselves, our Brethren, or the world. Justice is the cornerstone upon which we are instructed to erect our Masonic superstructure. For justice in a great measure constitutes the cement of all civil societies. Without it, universal confusion could reign, lawless force could replace equity, and social intercourse might be eliminated.

Through His wisdom, God has given us an opportunity to follow His plan for just relationships. A Freemason need look no farther than the Volume of the Sacred Law on how we may participate in His plan. If tempted to steal what belongs to another, we are to resist. If we give in to the temptation, we are to repay what was taken, make amends with our neighbor and sin no more. Man is tempted by many passions arising from lust, greed and vanity. Freemasons are taught that it is not only forbidden to grant control of oneself to one's passions, it is unjust.

To the law of God, Freemasonry adds an imperative contract obligation upon every Mason. Upon entering the Order, or fraternity, the initiate binds himself by a solemn vow to every other Mason in the world. The initiate becomes a brother to others he does not and may never know. He becomes responsible to families he may never see and to aid widows and orphans who are not yet widows or orphans. In essence he becomes obligated to people other than himself to whom he owes duties of kindness, sympathy and compassion.

In return for his vows, he is entitled to call upon every other Mason in the world for his assistance when in need, protection when in danger, sympathy when in sorrow, attention when ill, and a burial when dead. The reciprocal responsibilities, of the fraternity are emblematic of the just dues to be given as a standard or boundary of right to every man by every Mason.

A Freemason, while performing his just duties, is uniquely guided by the principles of impartially especially when acting toward other men, women and children without regard to their race, religion, creed, or political beliefs. It is not for the error in such beliefs or the different walks of life for which we chastise our brother (they are his beliefs and as such are his to hold), but for his intolerance of others and his lack charity towards all mankind.

Masons do not accuse fellow Brethren for believing in a different philosophy. We accuse a lack of kindness to others, a lack of sympathy, or a lack of integrity. Freemasons do not love their Brethren because they think alike but are loved simply because they are Brethren. And, we, as Masons, do not return an unkind act with yet another; we help to restore troubled souls with compassion.

Freemasons are expected to treat all human beings as brothers; especially those who are hateful, spiteful and wish everyone ill. All societies establish laws to guide the people who live within them. God, through the Volume of the Sacred Law, established laws for all to follow, regardless of the society within which one lives. Freemasonry extend its "laws," or rather its harmonious tenets, that every Mason may know that he is as much "at labor" outside of his Lodge as he is inside.

There was once a wise old man sitting at the gate of an ancient city. A young traveler stopped before entering the city and asked the old man, "What kind of people live in this town?" The wise man answered with a question, "What kind of people were in the town you just came from?" "Oh, they were liars and cheats and thugs and drunks, terrible people," the young traveler replied. The old man shook his head, "The people in this town are the same way." Later another stranger paused to ask the same question, and again the wise man questioned his questioner, "What kind of people did you just leave?" The second traveler answered, "Oh, I left a fine town. The people were good and kind and honest and hardworking." The wise man smiled and said, "The people in this town are the same way." People who are kind and forgiving toward others usually experience tolerance from others themselves; those who are harsh, censorious and critical toward others find that others exhibit much the same disposition toward them. (Harris, Robert. "Evaluating Internet Research Sources." Virtual Salt. 22 November 2010. Web. 20 Apr. 2011.)

Of course, when our Lord warned, "Judge not," He was not talking about exposing the sins of the ungodly—we must do that. Neither was He talking about withdrawing from the immoral, or restoring erring Masons, or resolving civil disputes, or "knowing a tree by its fruits." He was forbidding illegitimate judgments that stem from a self-righteous, haughty, puffed-up, hypocritical spirit (Matt. 7:15; Luke 6:37, 38; Rom. 2:1–3). He was forbidding judgments based on inadequate information (John 7:21–24). He was forbidding judgments in which the person assumes the position of God, trying and sentencing Brethren, in regard to eternal salvation (Josh. 4:11, 12; Rom. 14:3, 4, 10, 13; 1 Cor. 4:5). What kinds of Masons attend your Lodge? What kind of Mason are you electing to office in your Lodge?

As Freemasons, we are also taught to regard the laws of the land in which we respectively live as deserving of our complete and unhesitating devotion. Thus, it is not for the Freemason to pick and choose which laws to follow, but to follow all of them and make equal application of them all. Masons are expected to act for the preservation of freedoms whether in the form of public education, or the selection of houses of worship, and to judge each other by the extent of charity freely given. When given in a great measure, the good it serves is limitless. The old are comforted, the ill healed, orphans have fathers, widow are not alone, and God's justice is meted out to every man, woman, and child.

Thus, the verse, "Judge not lest ye be judged," has a double meaning for the Mason. He must measure his judgment of others with Diligence, Prudence, Temperance, and Discretion in balance with his own charity and wisdom from the Volume of the Sacred Law.

To illustrate this point, I am reminded about the boy who failed all his college work. He texted his mother; "Failed everything; prepare Papa." His mom texted back, "Papa prepared; prepare yourself." (Author Unknown)

Ruth E. Knowlton tells this on herself: "Years ago I lived in an apartment building in a large city. The building next door was only a few feet away from mine, and I could look across the alley into the apartment on the same floor as mine. There was a woman who lived there, whom I had never met, yet I could see her as she sat by her window each afternoon, sewing or reading. "After several months had gone by, I began to notice that her windows were dirty. Everything was indistinct through her smudged windows. I would say to myself, 'I wonder why that woman doesn't wash her windows? They look dreadful!' "One bright morning I decided to do my spring housecleaning and thoroughly cleaned my apartment, including washing the windows on the inside. "Late in the afternoon when I was finished, I sat down by the window with a cup of coffee for a rest. What a surprise! Across the way, the woman sitting by her window was clearly visible. Her windows were clean! "Then it dawned on me.

I have been criticizing her dirty windows, but all the time I was observing them through my own dirty ones!"

In most things we are reasonable enough to withhold judgment until we have examined them in their entirety. For instance, no man attempts to judge as to the vastness and grandeur of the ocean because he has seen a cup of its water; no man judges the beauty and strength of a building from a bit of the brick of which it is built, or of the purpose of the author from a word cut here and there from one of his books. When we look at our own lives, however, logic seems to weaken, and we draw the most unreasonable conclusions. We plunge into some dark cavern and lament, "Oh that all my labor and pains should have come to this! Oh, that God should have turned a deaf ear to my pleadings!" If we would wait long enough, we would see that we have been gently forced into the only avenue through which the light we asked for can be reached.

As Masons we sometimes fall into the trap of negative judging. Let us not be like that man who is always quick to judge his fellowmen: If he is poor, he is a bad manager. If he is rich, he is dishonest. If he needs credit, he can't get it. If he is prosperous, everyone wants a favor from him. If he's in politics, it's for pie. If he is out of politics, you can't place him, and he's no good for his country. If he doesn't give to charity, he's stingy. If he does, it's for show. If he is actively religious, he is a hypocrite. If he takes no interest in religion, he's a hardened sinner. If he shows affection, he's a soft specimen. If he seems to care for no one, he's cold-blooded. If he dies young, there was a great future ahead of him. If he lives to an old age, he has missed his calling. (From Edward Menkin, Attorney

At Law; Chicago printed on the back of his business card and reprinted in Law notes, Volume 11; July 1907, page 79).

Those who speak evil of others are usually too quick to draw conclusions. If they see a man coming out of a bar, they immediately decide he must have been drinking. They lack the charitable nature that would let them consider that he may very well have gone in to distribute Christian tracts in a place where they were desperately needed, or he may have gone in to try to persuade a weaker brother to leave the place and go home.

In closing I am reminded about a small orphaned boy lived with his grandmother. One night their house caught fire. The grandmother, trying to rescue the little boy asleep upstairs, perished in the smoke and flames. A crowd gathered around the burning house. The boy's cries for help were heard above the crackling of the blaze. No one seemed to know what to do, for the front of the house was a mass of flames. Suddenly a stranger rushed from the crowd and circled to the back where he spotted an iron pipe that reached an upstairs window. He disappeared for a minute, then reappeared with the boy in his arms. Amid the cheers of the crowd, he climbed down the hot pipe as the boy hung around his neck. Weeks later a public hearing was held in the town hall to determine in whose custody the boy would be placed. Each person wanting the boy was allowed to speak briefly. The first man said, "I have a big farm. Everybody needs the out-of-doors." The second man told of the advantages he could provide. "I'm a teacher. I have a large library. He would get a good education." Others spoke. Finally, the richest man in the community said, "I'm wealthy. I could give the boy everything mentioned tonight: farm, education, and more, including money and travel. I'd like him in my home." The chairman asked, "Anyone else like to say a word?" From the backseat rose a stranger who had slipped in unnoticed. As he walked toward the front, deep suffering showed on his face. Reaching the front of the room, he stood directly in front of the little boy. Slowly the stranger removed his hands from his pockets. A gasp went up from the crowd. The little boy, whose eyes had been focused on the floor until now, looked up. The man's hands were terribly scarred. Suddenly the boy emitted a cry of recognition. Here was the man who had saved his life. His hands were scarred from climbing up and down the hot pipe. With a leap the boy threw himself around the stranger's neck and held on for life. The farmer rose and left. The teacher, too. Then the rich man. Everyone departed, leaving the boy and his rescuer who had won him without a word. Those marred hands spoke more effectively than any words. ("Scarred Hands" (James S. Hewett, Illustrations Unlimited, pp. 119-120)

It is the actions of the Mason who lives by the justice and charity taught in this degree that has the scared hands from building his moral and Masonic edifice.

Chapter 8

Untempered Mortar

I happened to be at one of our jobsites today and noticed the brick masons scrambling around like a bunch of ants whose nest had just been disturbed. Our foreman came up and quietly informed me that we may have a problem with one of the rooms we were roughing out. As we walked toward the room, you couldn't help but overhear the brick mason superintendent climbing all over someone's case about the wall. I looked in amazement as the floor of the room was littered with eight by ten CMUs, short for cement masonry units or cement bricks. They were everywhere and the only thing left in the walls where they had been were the switch box and conduit, we were putting in.

It was then that I heard a term we use in lodge. The superintendent exclaimed to the young brick mason, "You used untempered mortar! I hope it's just this wall." With that the two left the area. There was nothing left for us to do except remove the box and conduit and wait on them to rebuild the wall so we could set the box and conduit in place again.

On the way home I got to thinking, which is unusual for me since it causes my hair to catch on fire and gives me a headache. Anyway, I was remembering the apron presentation by the Senior Warden as he tells the newly made brother, "not to daub with untempered mortar." Alright, what does that simple sentence really mean? How does it apply to us today?

In order to answer the question, we must first look at the terminology contained within the phrase. Daub is still used today by various trades, in the science arts and so forth. So, I looked it up and it means to coat or smear a surface with a thick or sticky substance in a carelessly rough or liberal way. As a noun, daub means plaster, clay, or another substance used for coating a surface, especially when mixed with straw and applied to laths or wattles to form a wall. Its synonyms are: smear, spread, coat, and soil.

Today we use one of the synonyms to affect the meaning of the word "daub". Ball players use spread, coat, put, and smear. If put on the baseball; by a player, the pitchers and umpires call it "Juicing" the ball and that's illegal. However, prior to being used in a game, MLB baseballs are rubbed with what is called Mississippi Mud and comes from a particular region of the Mississippi River. The mud on the banks of river has a certain mineral make up that is not found anywhere else in the world. They use it to take the sheen off the newly made baseballs, so they won't be slick. Cement masons call it "buttering" a brick or tile.

Do you find that we often "smear" or "daub" or even "juice" what we feel our lives should be in order to appear better than we are? Sometimes, more often than not, it is our ego or our pride that is doing that kind of talking instead of the honesty we were taught earlier in life. This can stem from falsely assuming that we need to measure up to someone else's expectations or a guilty feeling that we don't measure up to our own standards and expectations.

"Untempered" means "unmixed (in proper proportion)." In order for concrete to be strong, there must be the right amount of cement mixed with the water. If too much water is used, the concrete will be weak. If too much sand is used, the mixture lacks stability and is grainy. If too much cement mix is used the mixture becomes unstable and easily compresses into dust. By this definition of "untempered" we understand how the wall at the jobsite fell down. But in order to get a better view of the actual phrase used in the ritual we should take a look at the Scriptural reference it was derived from.

Ezekiel was a country prophet in captivity and had to contend with the false teachers in his day. The false prophets were prophesying out of their own hearts. They had seen nothing and were guilty of lying and divination, saying "The Lord said:" but the Lord had not sent them The Lord through Ezekiel described the false prophets as those who would daub a wall with untempered mortar: In verse 10b of Ezekiel chapter 13 we read, "One built up a wall, and, lo, others daubed it with untempered mortar: Say unto them which daub it with untempered mortar, that it shall fall: there shall be an overflowing shower; and ye, O great hailstones, shall fall; and a stormy wind shall rend it. Lo, when the wall is fallen, shall it not be said unto you, where is the daubing wherewith ye have daubed it?" (Ezekiel 13:10b – 12 KJV)

Now in consideration of the above scripture reference we can apply the second meaning of "untempered" which is "not moderated or controlled". If we look at the story in Ezekiel in its entirety, we find that Untempered Mortar has three characteristics.

First; it lacks stability. The Holy Word points out that the virtues and values of God are the prime ingredients for the mortar. The Freemason is charged with laying the proper foundation upon which to build his moral and Masonic edifice. The laying of that "cornerstone" has to be done with the proper Mortar of life. Without the proper mortar under his cornerstone the base will crumble and crack.

Second. It lacks strength and is weak. If your life values and virtues are not held together by those of God; and you are trusting in the wrong things of life; it is possible that the people you meet may be influenced by what you say and do. We as Masons are taught to edify and build up the people we interact with. We are taught to build our relationships with the Mortar contained within the Holy Word. Sadly, many have built their spiritual and moral walls the sloppy way. The good news is that we are warned not only of this as entered apprentices, but how to find the correct mix or recipe for our spiritual mortar which will help rebuild the moral walls.

And Thirdly; Untempered Mortar lacks security. As masons we are taught in the first degree that the lessons in life revolve around whom we place our trust in when we knelt for prayer and the lodge prayed for us. As we have seen in the episode of the wall at the jobsite; if we build a wall using the best bricks with untempered mortar, or the work isn't right, it will be for nothing and fall down. Many of us have built walls in the name of religion, masonry, ritual, good works and so on, but if that mortar, or work, is not properly mixed with the recipe from the values and teaching of the Holy Word, we will find our wall lying in a heap on the floor of life.

Erik X Briseño in his article, Untempered Mortar, for the Grand Lodge of Texas Masonic Education and Service Committee, says it this way: "To the speculative Mason, tampering with untempered mortar carries a most significant charge for new apprentices, and Freemasons. We must constantly prepare ourselves carefully, weighing our thoughts, actions, and deeds so as to create a spiritual temple that is stable, beautiful, and lasting. Each choice made in life is a part of that mixture, adding strength or weakness, as the case may be, to the character and reputation we have. Due attention must be paid to gaining and applying knowledge, acting wisely, and reflecting upon our spiritual journey as Masons."

He goes on to say, "As the apron protects our clothes from soiling, it is a reminder throughout the degrees, and evermore, that the purpose of the Craft is to achieve unity, peace, and happiness. Spotless conduct and character are goals, and the preparation and application of the mortar of Brotherly Love and Affection are what unite our Fraternity, now and forever." (Source URL: http://www.grandlodgeoftexas.org/node/171)

Sometimes in life we build our walls and our foundations with untempered things. Our egos and our pride often get in the way and we "daub" that wall or foundation with more "untempered" mortar to cover the sloppy workmanship we have allowed in our lives thus far. Masonry gently reminds us and shows us some practical ways to remove that mortar and replace it with a solid and properly mixed mortar so that our lives will reflect the good work our Father in Heaven has started in us.

In closing; let us, as Masons, remember the closing words of Charles H. Sprugeon's sermon The Wall Daubed With Untempered Mortar, (number 816) delivered on May 31, 1868 at the Metropolitan Tabernacle:

"If we build there, we shall build well, but if we build elsewhere, the great hailstones, and the overflowing shower and the total destruction will overwhelm us! As you remember this, may God help you to escape from ruin for Jesus' sake." (The C.H. Spurgeon Collection, Ages Software.)

CHAPTER 9

SQUARING OUR ACTIONS

I had just finished the construction progress meeting. While walking to the car, I happen to stop and watch the brick masons erect a wing wall. I was grabbed totally off guard when the foreman looked at me watching me and asked, "Have you ever wondered why we use the type of square we use?"

I must have looked like an idiot standing there with my mouth agape and replied in the most intellectual manor possible, "Huh?"

He walked up, introduced himself, then replied, "I saw your hat and I am a member of a Kansas Lodge. My family, we're all masons, both operative and speculative. Again, have you ever wondered why we use the square we use?"

"Hadn't ever noticed there was a difference. I assume that they were just like the ones I use or any other trade uses."

He studied me a bit and grabbed a "trying square", and a regular square, and said, "The try square has two arms of equal length that include an angle of 90°. It is not calibrated to measure lengths along the arms, because it is only used to test the angle between the two faces of a stone along the arris where they meet, to ensure that they subtend a right angle."

He continued, "But this square, look at it carefully, has no markings at all. It is used by fellow crafts to "square" their work. Notice how thick it is in relation to other squares and that it will not easily bend or be broken. We use it to prove how square the bricks or stones are before we can set them or "true" them up and ready them for use."

"Reminds me of some of the ritual in the lodge." I said and thanks for the Masonic education.

We parted and on the way to the office I thought about what I had seen and learned. How did it apply? What does it mean to square our actions? What is the Square of Virtue? And, why a square?

Masonically, the "square" has the same meanings we find outside of Masonry. (1) It is the conception of right-angled-ness. Our ritual says that the square is an angle of 90 degrees or the fourth part of a circle.

(2) The builder's tool, one of our working tools and it is the Master's Immovable Jewel according to some Masonic Jurisdictions.

And (3) According to: themasonictrowel.com/articles/degree_2nd_files/meaning _of_the_square, "The quality of character which has made "a square man" synonymous not only with a member of our fraternity, but with uprightness, honesty, and dependability."

References have been made all throughout history to the square's meaning as a symbol long before the start of Masonry as we know it. The Egyptians, Confucius and Aristotle refer to 'square actions.' They associate this with honest dealings, high morality and virtue. Even though the symbol is not a new symbol it has, throughout the ages, a remarkable consistency in its meaning along with the applications in practical uses.

Operative Masons use three types of squares; the square gauge, which is an enclosed square of the required inside dimensions to test a cubic ashlar or the cross section of a running stone. The try square, and the gallows square. The Gallows Square is used to set out right angles and has two arms of unequal length that include an angle of 90°. Both arms are calibrated on the inside and outside edges to facilitate the measurement of dimensions when scribing stones for cutting. It is also used to set out column bases, wall recesses and other details in the ground plans of structures. The usual sizes of gallows squares used in operative lodges were a small square in the ratio of 2:3 and having 12" x 18" arms; a general purpose square in the ratio of 3:4 called a Pythagorean square and having 18" x 24" arms; and a large square in the ratio of 2:3 and having 24" x 36" arms, which was used to check corners and other wall intersections both internally and externally.

Each has its own use for a specific task. Most of us are familiar with a Try-Square. It is usually found in woodworking but is also used by other trades. As we have discussed it is for marking and measuring a square piece of wood, metal or some other substance such as a brick or stone. The name refers to its primary use of measuring the accuracy of a right angle; to **try** a surface is to check its straightness or correspondence to an adjoining surface. In masonry when admitted for advancement as a Fellow craft in a speculative craft lodge the candidate is told that, having been obligated within the square, he is bound to act on the square to all mankind. This exhortation derives from the operative practice of requiring the candidate to kneel with both knees bare on an ashlar stone that was placed within the square gauge. The reason for the change is not recorded, but the present method of supporting the candidate's elbow within the angle of a small Pythagorean square was substituted for the operative practice at about the time when reconciliation between the Antients and the Moderns was achieved. The traditional "Square and Compasses" emblem should incorporate a try square that has not been calibrated and a similar square should also be used to form the emblem representing the three great emblematic lights of freemasonry. Because the try square is used to test the angles of a perfect ashlar stone, it is a universal emblem of morality and justice that inculcates truthfulness, honesty and a strict obedience to the law of God's Word. It therefore is rightfully included in the three great emblematic lights by which we shall be tried as "living stones". In Isaiah 28:16 of the New English Bible we read:

"These then are the words of the Lord God: look, I am laying a stone in Zion, a

block of granite, a precious cornerstone for a firm foundation; he who has faith

shall not waver".

Psalm 118:22 also says that "The stone which the builders rejected has become the chief cornerstone."

With arms in the 3:4 or Pythagorean ratio, we find the gallows square as the traditional emblem of the Master that has been used from time immemorial by operative freemasons. We also found that the gallows square is used to set out the work, which, in today's lodges, is the Master's duty, so it has become the most appropriate square to use as the emblem of the Master's office. In England, for some reason, apparently during the 1830s after Euclid's 47th

Proposition was introduced as the basis of the speculative Past Master's jewel, the speculative Master's emblem was changed to a try square. Perhaps this was a result of the early speculative ritualists' passion for symmetry.

We have taken a look at the various squares used in the craft trades as well as in our lodges. Scripture reminds us to be upright and true while practicing the tenants of our institution. Thus we can see through the use of various squares how Masonry has been influenced by their design and their use in the skilled trades. So now when you go into your home shop, you might be reminded of the principles by which they were designed and keep their instructions close to our heart.

CHAPTER 10
WHY BY THE SQUARE?

Having been a District Deputy Grand Lecturer we have a tendency to concentrate on the words of the ritual and not the meaning of those words. Yes, I am guilty of the same thing. I can remember sitting in the lodges in my district and correcting the Senior Warden when asked "why by the Square?" The responses, over the course of my masonic career as a lecturer, have been enlightening to say the least, however, we still must ask, Why by the Square?

I sat in Temperance Lodge # 438 and listened as the Senior Warden gave a perfect answer to the question, which starts off …BECAUSE. It's like my parents when we would be corrected and ask why. They would always say "BECAUSE I SAID SO." Remember those famous sayings? And most of them started with the same word – because. Was a ritual writer of long ago angry with his student and started that sentence with "Because?" Or is it due to the continuation of an explanation that started in the Entered Apprentice Degree?

In the Entered Apprentice Degree, the mason is taught that the square is one of the great lights of our Fraternity. As a Fellowcraft he learns that is a working tool and is to be used a certain way. As a fellowcraft he learns that squaring your work is a vital and important part of making sure that the stones making up the edifice are correct and true. In the Master Mason degree, we learn the importance of forming a square. Let's take a look at some of the meanings of the square. We learned in Chapter 9 what a Square is and what types there are now we will look at the Masonic symbolism and what, we as Masons, should learn from them.

A few keywords on "square" as a symbol include Grounding, Stabilizing, Structure, Foundation, Basics, Community, Elemental, Balance, Pragmatic, Direction, Dependability, and Integrity. One such meaning according to Rowena and Rupert Shepherd in their book, 1000 Symbols: What Shapes Mean in Art and Myth; a square is a symbol of the heart in Islam. Each side of the heart-square symbolizes an aspect or opening for awareness and inspiration: i.e. Angelic, Diabolic, Human, and Divine.

Remember the Atari game Pong? That little ball you could bounce between two parallel lines (presumably representing a ping-pong paddle). Our awareness can be that point bouncing between the aspects of duality housed within each side of our experience (dark, light, up, down, physical, spiritual, etc.).

We can branch off from there by observing the four-sided structures that surround us in our environment. Like: The four cardinal directions (north, south, east, west). The four major seasons (winter, spring, summer, autumn). The four cosmic elements (suns, moons, planets, stars). The four common phases of human life (birth, child, adult, death). The four prime elements (fire, earth, air, water). In the Kabbalah it means "Spirit/God hidden in matter." And the list can go on and on depending on your faith, social upbringing, education, etc.

The Square and compasses, one of the most common symbols of Freemasonry, are architect's tools, and to some symbolize God as the architect of the universe, among other things. As measuring instruments, the tools represent judgment and discernment. The compasses, which is used to draw circles, can represent the realm of the spiritual - eternity. It can be symbolic of a defining and limiting principle, and also of infinite boundaries. To some the angle measures the square, the symbol of earth and the realm of the material.

Based on some of the explanations we have given, and through the adoption and expansion of these explanations through history; the square represents fairness, balance, firmness, etc., which is reflected in phrases such as "on the square" and "squared away." Something that is squared is something that is stable, a foundation for building upon.

W.Bro. Kent Henderson, Past Junior Grand Deacon, A. F. & A. Masons of Victoria, Australia; in his article titled "A JOURNEY THROUGH THE SECOND DEGREE" states:

"In the Second Degree the Lodge is opened on the Square that great Masonic emblem of the Golden Rule, of doing unto others as in similar cases we would wish that they should do to us. or as we Freernasons put it, of acting on the Square. this is the way of life that Freemasonry teaches, and has ever taught, that is, to so harmonize our conduct in this life as to render us acceptable to that Divine Being, from whom all goodness springs, It is thus fitting that the candidate for the Second Degree should gain admission by the assistance of the Square."

He further states: "In the earliest known Masonic catechism there is this question: "How many make a Lodge?" and the answer is given as: "God and the Square, and five or seven right or perfect

Masons". This sounds like a riddle, but it is easily explained. "God and the Square": knowing the meaning of the Square, we are immediately reminded of the Fatherhood of God and the Brotherhood of man. To love God and our neighbor is to keep all the commandments, which, of course, is what Christ meant when he said, "On these two commandments hang all the law and the prophets." And now for the rest of the answer: "with five or seven right or perfect Masons". Five is right and seven is perfect, because "five hold a lodge" and so five is the right number to form a Masonic quorum; and seven is perfect because, as the First Tracing Board tells us: that is the number of "regularly made Masons, without which number no lodge is perfect".

Mackey's Revised Encyclopedia of Freemasonry, Volume 2, Page 963, 1929, A Short History About the Square and Compasses, says: THE SQUARE...Morality.

Throughout history, correctly or incorrectly, man has been guided by what he believes more so than what he knows – by faith more than reason. When you examine what has happened in your life, you may be able to agree with this statement. However, few take the time to determine whether what he believes has been proven to be accurate. If we study and apply all that is taught as a fellowcraft, we will acquire all the skills necessary to improve upon our talent to exercise morality, truthfulness, and virtue. Coupled with this we learn and understand how to use reason and love.

The Holy Bible lies open upon our Altar of Masonry, and upon the Bible lays the Square and Compasses. They are the three Great Lights of the Lodge. We can relate it as the Divine warrant and chief working tools. Together they work as symbols of Revelation, Righteousness and Redemption, teaching us that by walking in the light of Truth, and obeying the Law contained within the Volume of Sacred Law, the Divine in man wins victory over the earthly.

Concentrating on how to live is the one important matter we find as a constant theme in all the degrees of Masonry, and sometimes the mason will search far and wide looking for a wiser and better way, but not being able to find a better tool than that shown us by the Great Lights of the Lodge.

"To properly form the angle of the square, it is absolutely essential that we practice, practice, and practice yet again so that reason and love become as habitual to our behavior, as faith is to our spiritual nature." (Advanced Meditations on Masonic Symbolism by John R. Heisner , (Publish America) page 69.)

Because…it is an Emblem of Virtue…

"Virtues" are morally good habits of acting which reside in individual souls. Cardinal comes from carde, Latin for "hinge." In traditional Catholic philosophy all other virtues hinge, turn or depend on four cardinal virtues because they describe the fundamental structures of health of the soul. First clearly formulated by Plato in The Republic, repeated and expanded by Aristotle, they became a classical commonplace and were adopted by all major medieval philosophers. They are also mentioned in Scripture in the deutero-canonical, or apocryphal, Book of Wisdom of Solomon.

Their basis is in human nature itself, in the soul, which directs bodily actions in its three parts or functions. First, intelligence, or reason, is perfected by the virtue of prudence, or practical wisdom.

Second, will is perfected by the virtue of fortitude, or courage. Third, appetites are perfected by the virtue of moderation, or self-control (sophrosyne, there is no good English equivalent to this Greek notion, with its strong aesthetic overtones of harmony and beauty). The fourth and overarching virtue, justice, is the harmony, integration and correct functioning of the three parts. Rightness or righteousness might be closer to the original meaning, for justice connotes to the modern mind almost exclusively social justice, fairness in relations between individuals rather than right relations within a single individual, that is, among parts of the soul.

The cardinal moral virtues are distinguished from the intellectual virtues, or virtues of the speculative intellect (wisdom, science and understanding), and both are distinguished, as natural virtues, from the three supernatural or "theological virtues" which have God as their object: faith, hope and charity.

Phil. 4:8 tells us: "Whatsoever things are true, whatsoever things are honest, whatsoever things are just, whatsoever things are pure, whatsoever things are of good report; if there be any virtue, and if there be any praise, think on these things."

While his own life may have fallen far short of the ideals of virtue, Benjamin Franklin was certainly right when he wrote, "There was never yet a truly great man that was not at the same time truly virtuous." We cannot then completely agree with the man who said, "great men have great faults." While some believe only Jesus Christ was perfect, true greatness must be built upon character and integrity.

Looking at this subject from a Pastor's perspective we learn in the Greek the expression: arête (Pronunciation: ahr eh TAY) means Virtuous.

We have all heard it said, "he is a virtuous man" or "she is a virtuous woman." Such comments are praises of a person's moral character. The Greek word for "virtuous" is aretē; it was used all the time in Greek literature, but only rarely in the New Testament.

Though "virtue" is said to have been possessed by various people, it is a quality that comes from God. In his first letter Peter used aretē to describe the excellent nature or "excellencies" of God (1 Pet. 2:9). In his second epistle, Peter uses "virtue" three times in the opening chapter. The first instance is in 2 Peter 1:3, where there is a significant textual variant. Some manuscripts indicate that the believers are called "by" God's glory and virtue; others indicate that they are called "to" God's glory and virtue. The first reading denotes that we are attracted by God's glory and virtue as expressed in Jesus Christ to follow Christ and become like Him. This reading suggests the means by which the divine call is exercised in our lives. The "virtues" refer to the qualities in Jesus which attracts believers to Him. The glory (doxa) which John saw in Jesus (John 1:14) was His authority and power; that which Peter saw probably refers to the Transfiguration, described in 2 Peter 1:16-18. Jesus' virtue (aretē) is that moral excellence which so continually awed His disciples.

The second reading means that we are called by God to participate in His very own glory and virtue. The rest of the passage in 2 Peter 1 primarily affirms the second reading—because this section tells us that we have been given God's divine power so that we can become partakers of His divine nature. One significant feature of the divine nature is "virtue." From this meaning from the New Testament it shows us that Masons, Christians, and others cannot produce this from themselves; it comes from the divine nature, of which we can partake by means of the Spirit of God.

Because… we can, if we so choose, make the connection that since the Square is placed on the Volume of Sacred Law, maybe, just maybe we should square our actions by the Volume of Sacred Law, which becomes our "Square of Virtue."

CHAPTER 11
The Masonic Blue Slipper

Stinging cold rain left small marks of red on her drenched face. Ms. McDean was doing her best to cover them and protect them both from the frigid onslaught that was blowing harder as they traveled about New England looking for the hotel that had eluded them. Wanting to escape the prevailing north wind and the pelting rain they ducked into a small, albeit friendly, English looking pub where the patrons looked on with curiosity.

The bar tender greeted them warmly and showed them a table next to the fireplace where they could dry out some and relax.

"What can I get ya ladies?" the barkeep inquired, all the while helping with the coats and hanging them near the fire so they would dry out also. Then he spotted it, the small blue pin. He looked and studied the small blue pin on the lapels of the drenched mother and daughter. He couldn't help but wonder.

"Coffee or tea would be fine for me and my daughter would like some tea as well. Thanks."

Ms. McDean had been widowed for some time having lost her husband to cancer several years back. She and her daughter, Jennifer, had been traveling the Northeast in fulfillment of a desire and a much-needed vacation. A stately looking woman when not drenched by rain, did not show her seven decades of living through some of the roughest times in life. Jennifer, now in her fifties, carried on the travel tradition with Ms. McDean.

"Here you go; two hot teas and some pastries on the house. I was wondering if I might be able to join you and visit for a while. I noticed your pins and would like to know more about them." John, the barkeep, made sure to flash his Masonic ring when he sat down the tea.

"Sure, I will be happy to explain the pin. But, first tell why you wear the ring that you do."

John pulled out one of the oak curved back chairs and sat at the round table with his back against the wall. His strapping features reminded Jennifer of an ex-marine or army veteran.

"Well, my name is John and I am currently Master of Hamlet Lodge number 110 here is this quaint little village and I wear my ring because I am a Mason and do my best to live by the principles taught by the fraternity."

"Well said," Ms. McDean replied. "My late husband was a doctor and brought this pin home for me and one for Jennifer several years before he died. He was a good man and his temperament was even keel and calm, much like yours. Charles was his name and he always made sure we were taken care of and allowed us to travel all over even if he couldn't join us.

"Charles was a Mason also and was a Past Master of his lodge as well. He loved the lodge and all it stood for. He would go help another brother at the drop of a hat and just lived the obligations he took as a Mason. He passed several years ago after a battle with cancer. So, whenever I travel I wear the pin he gave me."

"I see." Said John, "But what does it mean."

"John," she continued. "How well do you remember your initiation into lodge? And how well do you know your ritual?"

"Geez, I don't know it that well, but I do remember some key things."

"Let me start at the beginning about the pin. Let us go back in history to Boaz' time in the Book of Ruth. It will be remembered that Elimelech, his wife, Naomi, and their two sons, Mahlon and Chilon, fled to the land of Moab to escape the famine in their homeland of Bethlehem-Judah. Things went well for a while. Then life fell apart for them. Elimelech died and his two sons married Moabite girls- Orpha and Ruth. Again, tragedy struck. Mahlon and Chilon died. This left Naomi a widow in a foreign land with two widowed daughters-in-law from the land of Moab.

"In time of trouble, people think of home and more importantly of God. Naomi found out that the famine back home had subsided, and there was grain and food again. So, she confided with Orpha and Ruth that she would journey back home and be among her kinsmen. Certain laws, rules, or customs governed her thinking at this time. Of first consideration was the fact that Naomi was too old to bear a son for her daughters-in-law to marry. Even if she could, the daughters-in-law would not wait for the son to grow up. So, the girls should remain among their own people. The girls resisted and started to go with Naomi. Orpha was finally convinced she should stay in Moab. But Ruth remained steadfast and went with Naomi to her homeland.

Naomi and Ruth arrived back in Bethlehem-Judah at harvest time. The Scripture passage on which this is based is well known. And Ruth said, "Entreat me not to leave thee, or to return from following after thee: for whither thou goest, I will go; and where thou lodgest, I will lodge: thy people shall be my people, and thy God my God: Where thou deist, will I die, and there will I be buried: the Lord do so to me, and more also, if ought but death part thee and me." (Ruth 1:16-18 KJV) This passage of Scripture is unsurpassed as a declaration of love and devotion of one person for another. It has been said that it would make a good marriage vow. But, to me it is a different type of devotion.

"Naomi also had to take into consideration another law. When Elimelech died, his next of kin was duty bound to redeem his possessions and take care of his widow and her family. Since Naomi was getting old, Ruth tried to earn a livelihood. While gleaning in the fields, she was seen by Boaz. And when he found out about her (that she was Naomi's daughter-in-law, etc.), he arranged special treatment for her. She could work with his girls in the field, and the young men were warned not to bother her. Since Boaz was not married and was kin to Naomi, Naomi decided that she should somehow make Boaz understand his duty to Elimelech's family. So, Naomi advised Ruth to bathe and anoint herself and go to the threshing floor after dark and lay at the feet of Boaz. Boaz awoke at midnight and discovered her there. So as not to create a scandal, he gave her some barley and asked her to leave before dawn so that watching eyes would not recognize her.

"Business among the tribe of Bethlehem-Judah took place at the gate of the city. So, Boaz sat down at the gate the next day because he knew there was a kinsman more closely related to Elimelech than he. So, when the kinsman came by, Boaz called him aside and asked 10 men of the elders of the city to sit with them. Boaz bargained with his kinsman. The kinsman said he would redeem Elimelech's property. But, when he found out that he would have to take care of Naomi and Ruth, he reneged and told Boaz he would not redeem or protect Elimelech's interest. He would leave it to Boaz. The passage from Scripture for these events is this: "And the kinsman said, I cannot redeem it for myself, lest I mar mine own inheritance: redeem thou my right to thyself; for I cannot redeem it. Now this was the manner in former time in Israel concerning redeeming and concerning changing, for to confirm all things; a man plucked off his shoe and gave it to his neighbor: and this was a testimony in Israel."

"So the kinsman drew off his shoe and gave it to Boaz. Boaz held it up for all in the gate to see. He asked them to be witnesses that he became Naomi's protector, Ruth's husband, and a redeemer of Elimelech's property."

John's look of bewilderment asked the question his lips were too afraid to vocalize.

"John," She continued. "Charles told me that during the initiation of a candidate, one slipper is on and one is off and that the meaning behind this is explained in the first-degree lecture. Not having been through the degrees I must take my husband at his word. He informed me that the pin is in the shape of that blue slipper to remind fellow masons of their obligations. It has the Square and Compasses to denote that the wearer is Masonically related. The color of blue, signifies the perfection of Deity and the gold laurel represents the pureness of heart and the sacredness of personal sacrifice.

"The pin was originally developed in the 1930' s, and although the original inventor and maker has escaped recorded history, we find its use in today's masonry less prominent than in earlier years.

"I might mention that this pin has always been known as the "Widows Pin" and because of that, I have always been treated very well and honestly throughout the years by every Mason I have met while traveling. It was because of the protective influence that Masons have for their wives, widows, and daughters that the pin was developed."

"Thank you for your time and the explanation of the pin. I had never seen one as unique as that one is. I would like to find some of these and give them to our wives at an open meeting." John said. "Oh, by the way, where were you to going?"

"To the Hamlet Inn, but we got lost in the storm."

"It is two blocks down the street. I take you there myself. Ya know," he continued, "God has a unique way sometimes of spreading the message of Brotherly Love, Relief, and Truth."

This story was adopted from an article written by Clyde H. Magee, 32° in the July 1986 issue of the New Age Journal or Scottish Rite Journal. All Scripture quotations from the Book of Ruth are from the Authorized Version of the King James Bible.

CHAPTER 12

THE TABERNACLE

A masonic lodged is situated due East and West, because after Moses had conducted the Children of Israel through the Red Sea (Sea of Reeds), he, by divine command, erected a Tabernacle in the Wilderness, which he placed due East and West, to commemorate that mighty east wind which brought their miraculous deliverance. A pattern of the Tabernacle was exhibited to Moses at Mount Sinai. This modified version of the description is from the First Degree Lecture from the Grand Lodge of Missouri.

The Tabernacle and its construction is found primarily in Exodus; and Hebrews 8:5; 9:24 of the Great Light of Masonry. It is true that the design and layout, as portrayed in the Missouri Ritual, was given to Moses on Mount Sinai (Exodus 25:2, 8-9, 40; and Hebrews 8:5; 9:24). This occurred after the Children of Israel had been led out of Egypt and they followed God as a pillar of fire and a pillar of smoke until they reached the mountain of God where they camped for several years.

During the time of the construction of the tabernacle, Moses built a "tent of meeting" outside the camp so he could privately enter into the God's presence or Shekinah Glory and receive divine guidance and answers to the people's prayers (Exodus 33:7-11). This tent was a provisional structure that was later incorporated into the tabernacle, since the terms tent of meeting and tabernacle are used interchangeably after the tabernacle's completion (Leviticus 1:3;

Deuteronomy 31:14-15). Samuel also noted God's movements in 2 Samuel 7:6 by saying, "God moved about in a tent, even in a tabernacle." Years later when Solomon's temple was completed and dedicated, the portable tent of meeting/tabernacle and its sacred vessels were incorporated into the temple (1 Kings 8:4). The picture below is the inside of the Tabernacle. [7]

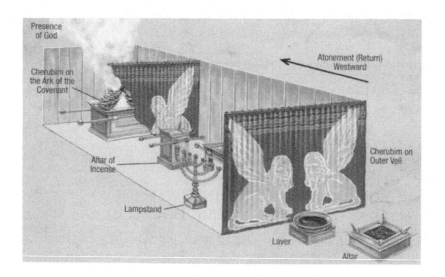

The Tabernacle was 30 Cubits (45 feet) in Length by 10 Cubits (15 feet) Wide. The Holy place was 20 Cubits (30 feet) by 10 Cubits (15 feet) and the Holy of Holies was 10 Cubits by 10 Cubits. I thought I would mention here that if we look at the layout of the Tabernacle; notice that the Holy of Holies is in the West not the East. Some Masonic scholars have placed the Holy of Holies in the East.

---

[7] 2012 Bristol Works, Inc. Rose Publishing, Inc. Illustration by Cara Nilsen Page 8, used by permission.

The layout of the Tabernacle and the layout of the Temple were identical in the placement of the Holy Place and the Holy of Holies. This is contrary to opinions held by some scholars and theologians.

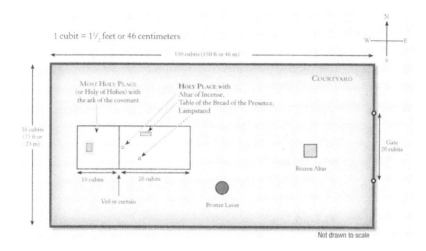

The above picture[8] shows the relationship of the Tabernacle within the Courtyard which has only one entry or exit gate. The walls of the courtyard consisted of wooden pillars spaced about 10 feet apart and between the pillars was a fabric wall. The Tabernacle was covered with four layers of fabric, consisting of a layer of fine linen, a layer of wool, a layer of Angora goat hair and a heavy layer of rough goat hair which is the same for all top layers of tents.

There is not enough time to explain the various materials used in the construction of the Tabernacle and why. Suffice it to say that Silver, which was used for the sockets which held the posts for the

---

[8] 2012 Bristol Works, Inc. Rose Publishing, Inc.

plank walls, Gold which covered the plank walls and was used for other items, Jewels which adorned the Breast plate and other sacred objects, and finally Bronze which was used for the Altar and the Laver among other things. What is interesting to note is that God required of each individual one silver coin, which came from the plunder of Egypt when they left.

Nearly 300 verses in Exodus are devoted to an account of the Tabernacle and its furniture, while the corresponding account of the Temple and its furniture in First Kings and Second Chronicles, is comprised of half that number of verses.

Many of the words, phrases and terms we use today and especially in Masonry have arisen from, or are illustrated by, the tabernacle and it rites. Here are a few examples: Veil, Mercy Seat, Propitiation, Laver of Regeneration, Lamb of God, Washed, Cleansed, Purged, Reconciled, Sacrifice, Offering, and Atonement. Keep in mind that the book of Exodus is the most picturesque book of the Bible. It contains more word pictures than any other book in the Bible.

The tabernacle served God's purpose as a sanctuary for 485 years (from Moses to Solomon). Its purpose was to make possible God's dwelling with his people. It was made to be an earthly copy of the heavenly sanctuary. Because of sin, God could not physically coexist with humans. Dwelling with God was only possible if there was a proper separation (the curtains of the tabernacle), a sanctified place of meeting (the Ark of the Covenant within the Holy of Holies), and a qualified mediator (the High Priest).

Bezalel and Oholiab were the two craftsmen along with Moses, whom God gave the details of the structure and the rules of ritual purification that maintained its sanctity to. These men were divinely appointed to supervise the skilled workers in making the structural framework, tent curtains, and ritual furniture. God instructed the priests how to conduct the divine service and how to prevent ritual desecration. Also, the people were told how to live godly lives that would sustain them collectively as a priestly nation. The materials mostly came from voluntary contributions except for the one silver coin and were a part of the plunder.

The tabernacle was situated in the middle of the twelve tribes of Israel. This location for the tabernacle was necessary because it served as the focal point of Israel's daily life. In this way, God, whose presence was manifested at the tabernacle as a cloud of smoke and a pillar of fire, was continually at the center of his people. Notice how this same principle is used in our lodges. The Great Light of Masonry is placed on the altar, which is located in the center of the lodge room, so that all may see its illumination and instruction.

As I have stated earlier about the placement of the Holy of Holies, do you find it an interesting curiosity that as the sun rises in the East it is shining upon the Holy of Holies. Our candidates are raised in the west end of the lodge where the Sanctum Sanctorum would be if the lodge room copied the layout of the temple. Notice that the ritual says "As near the Sanctum Sanctorum as Jewish law would permit."

The tabernacle was laid out so that traveling in a westerly direction within the tabernacle was to travel towards Atonement or closeness with God and traveling in an easterly direction was to travel away from the same. We see this same pattern in the layout of the Garden of Eden. The Tree of Life was in the western portion of the Garden and the entry gate, guarded by the two Cherubim and flaming sword, was in the east.

From a Masonic point of view, these patterns, could have significant application to each religion represented in Masonry. My knowledge is limited to only those of the Christian and Jewish faith. If we take a look at some of the most significant religious churches and temples in the world, we see this same pattern repeated. I found an interesting fact that the sockets used for the walls and tent covering were numbered from 1 to 100. Guess where socket one was located? You guessed it – in the North East corner. Coincidence? Maybe, but I offer up that this knowledge of the layout of structure was passed down from generation to generation. It would make sense and fit that the first stone of your Masonic and Moral edifice be placed in the Northeast Corner.

I hope this brief explanation of the Tabernacle gives you a cause to explore not only our ritual in Masonry, the ritual used by your Church, and especially studying the Great Light of Masonry and what it teaches. For it is by the studying of the Great Light that we fulfill our motto of making "Good Men Better."

For further reading and the study of the Tabernacle consult, "Rose Guide to The Temple" Rose Publishing company and "The Tabernacle, its priests and its services" by William Brown; Henderson Publishing.

CHAPTER 13
THE WORDS WE USE

Words; are the most powerful force in all of creation. How powerful are words? Listen to what the Supreme Architect of the Universe says in Genesis 1:3 (KJV) "And God Said…" Again, in John 1: 1 (KJV) we find, "In the beginning was the Word, and the Word was with God, and the Word was God." Those two verses demonstrate how powerful words are.

With words we can turn a man into a degraded, blubbering shell of what was once someone with integrity, fortitude and fidelity. Or with words we can plant the seeds of greatness which will benefit all mankind. One unintentional phrase can destroy a solidly built nation or destroy the dreams of a child. A well-placed phrase can unite a nation or place a man on the moon. They can build up or destroy and they can encourage or incriminate. A phrase can inspire or leave a person emotionally flat. James reminds us in James 1:26 (NIV) "If anyone considers himself religious and yet does not keep a tight rein on his tongue, he deceives himself and his religion is worthless." So how do you use the words you have learned?

All of our tenets and cardinal virtues have one common thread. They contain words which can be used in any manor you choose. The words explaining Brotherly Love, Relief and Truth; if properly used with meaning, can inspire future generations of Masons. Yet, they can without our knowledge, destroy the credibility we have worked so hard to build. When said without feeling, leave the intended emotionless and empty, questioning whether he should have joined our fraternity. We display the tenets of our institution best by the words we use and by the way we say them.

Romans 10:17 (KJV) says, "So then faith cometh by hearing, and hearing by the word of God." If we take a look at the first part of the verse, we can apply it to our daily lives in the way we use our words. A new candidate will hear the faith we have in our great institution by the way we say the words contained within our ritual. He will understand Brotherly Love by the way we address and talk with our fellow brethren. 70% of all verbal communication comes from the tones and the way we say the words we use. A candidate will not remember all of what was said but, he will remember the way we said it. The feeling we use in saying our ritual can reflect the belief we have in our ritual and in our fraternity.

To demonstrate this; think of a movie you really enjoy watching. How do the actors portray what is happening? They use feeling and emotion to communicate with their words. Now, imagine what that same movie would be like if those same words in the same scene were just words, a monotone of saying the script. Would the impact of the scene be the same? I think not. Think about the Good Ritualists verses the Great Ritualists? In your own district and regions, I am sure you can distinguish the difference. What is that difference since most are ritualistic near perfect with the wording? Isn't it the delivery; the way they said those same words?

Ritual, when said with feeling, creates excitement and enthusiasm for what we are saying. In turn this reflects the passion we have for our beloved fraternity. To give you a great example of how powerful putting feeling into ritual is let me tell a small story. The Royal Arch degree is a retelling of the 2nd building of King Solomon's Temple according to the book of Ezra as found in the Old Testament. During the ritual, the candidate takes a journey back to Israel to help in the reconstruction. A character called the Principle Sojourner, for those of you who have not gone through the York Rite yet; the officer performs the same function as a Senior Deacon and is the main character. He conducts the candidate through his journey explaining various truths as found along the way. I had the rare privilege of having RWB Quisenberry be the Principle Sojourner when I went through a York Rite Festival in Independence. There were about 25 in our class. Every one of them said they felt as if they were actually on the journey and could imagine the setting.

What made that impression? It was feeling and passion. His delivery made all the difference in the world. It brought the ritual to life. In the Second Section of the 3rd Degree are we not in the same position? Consider the condition of the candidate and the great moral lesson contained within the degree. If we do not add feeling in this portion of our ritual, in what condition will we find the candidate at the appropriate time? Will he be alert or asleep? Will he have pictured in his mind the story portrayed? Will he have felt the passion and love for the one he represents by his fellow brethren and will the lessons be implanted in his mind?

We have three lectures in Blue Lodge. Each one is a conversation with the candidate or candidates as the case may be. Those of us who have them committed to memory need to consider our delivery. Contained within each lecture is a host of great moral truths and it is our duty to convey those truths to the best of our ability. If we just say the words our candidate will walk away with the feeling of emptiness. However, if we say it as a conversation or telling the story, our candidate will learn, and we will have accomplished our goal of imprinting on the mind wise and serious truths.

I submit to you my brethren to consider how we say our ritual. Not all of us are actors but, we all have our own personalities. By putting our own feelings and allowing our individual personalities be reflected in the ritual, not only are we going to inspire others to learn and participate, but, we will make an impression and demonstrate the great Masonic tenet of Brotherly Love and Affection.

CHAPTER 14

THE LION OF THE TRIBE OF JUDAH

Third degrees in Masonry can produce many interesting questions and inspire newly made masons and older masons on a search that can change their lives forever. Some don't even know what questions to ask because you cannot ask questions about that which you do not know. Most of us don't know what we don't know so we can't even begin to formulate a list of questions on things we don't know. However, one sharp candidate in St. Joseph came to me not long ago and ask a question that I hadn't thought about or researched since Seminary.

"RW Sir," he began, "in the prayer that was said when I got my third degree the chaplain referred to the Lion of the Tribe of Judah. I was wondering if that was the same as King Solomon?"

Interesting question and probably many have thought the same thing. Some lodges have a picture of a Lion on a banner in a corner as part of the York Rite rituals and some have just a Lion lying next to a Lamb in a meadow. Most of us have seen the latter of these two in one form or another. The question now is raised as to how the two relate; or better yet why it relates to Masonry.

Remember in the Third degree we have two prayers and the second one is most commonly used in our area of the state. The last line of this prayer reads "…we may meet that hour in the glad hope that even Death itself shall surrender its hold at the magic touch of the "Lion of the Tribe of Judah", and His strong grip shall raise us to enter into everlasting rest and refreshment in the Grand Lodge on High." My obligation does not allow me to expand on the other use of the phrase "Lion of the Tribe of Judah." Suffice it to say that it is contained in the Third degree and is very significant.

Let's take a look at where the name "Lion of the Tribe of Judah" came from. The actual term comes from the Holy Bible and can be found in Revelation Chapter 5:2-5. "John saw a mighty angel and heard him ask in a loud voice, who is worthy to break the seals and open the scroll?"

The Greek word rendered "scroll" is **biblion**, from which is derived the word "Bible."

"When no one was found to be worthy, John wept and wept (lit., "kept on shedding many tears"). One of the 24 elders, however, told him not to weep, and introduced him to the **Lion of the tribe of Judah**, the Root of David (cf. Isa. 11:1; Rev. 22:16). The elder informed John that He had triumphed, that is, had already achieved victory, and that He alone was able to break the seals and open the scroll." (The Bible Knowledge Commentary: An Exposition of the Scriptures by Dallas Seminary Faculty.)

The actual phrase has its roots in a prophecy found in Isaiah 11:1-12 (NIRV)

"Jesse's family is like a tree that has been cut down. A new little tree will grow from its stump. From its roots a Branch will grow and produce fruit. This is the main part of the prophecy that the prayer refers to or has it as the root of Revelation 5:5.

Verse 2 continues the prophecy: "The Spirit of the LORD will rest on that Branch. He will help him to be wise and understanding. He will help him make wise plans and carry them out. He will help him know the LORD and have respect for him. The Branch will take delight in respecting the LORD. He will not judge things only by the way they look. He won't make decisions based simply on what people say. He will always do what is right when he judges those who are in need. He'll be completely fair when he makes decisions about poor people. When he commands that people be punished, it will happen. When he orders that evil people be put to death, it will take place. He will put godliness on as if it were his belt. He'll wear faithfulness around his waist. Wolves will live with lambs. Leopards will lie down with goats. Calves and lions will eat together. And little children will lead them around. Cows will eat with bears. Their little ones will lie down together. And lions will eat straw like oxen. A baby will play near a hole where cobras live. A young child will put his hand into a nest where poisonous snakes live. None of those animals will harm or destroy anything or anyone on my holy mountain of Zion. The oceans are full of water. In the same way, the earth will be filled with the knowledge of the LORD. At that time the man who is called the Root from Jesse's family line will be like a banner that brings nations together. They will come to him. And the place where he rules will be glorious."

The above portion of the prophecy is what generated, among other verses, the Lion and the Lamb painting commonly used in some Masonic rituals outside the third degree.

Continuing with verse 11; "At that time the LORD will reach out his hand to gather his people a second time. He will bring back those who are left alive. He'll bring them back from Assyria, Lower Egypt, Upper Egypt and Cush. He'll bring them from Elam, Babylonia and Hamath. He will also bring them from the islands of the Mediterranean Sea."

The reason for the banner in the York Rite and Scottish Rite can be found in verse 12; "He will lift up a banner. It will show the nations that he is gathering the people of Israel. He'll bring back those who had been taken away as prisoners. He'll gather together the scattered people of Judah. He'll bring them back from all four directions."

We see here why the founding fathers of Masonic ritual might have chosen this as the basis for so much of the rituals in various additional degrees. Now back to the original question as to who it is. We actually find the answer to this question later on in Revelation. As you ponder this little lesson keep in the back of your mind that there is only one reference to the "Lion of the Tribe of Judah" in all of Scripture. Isaiah 11:1 is the basis for Revelation 5:5 which establishes the Root of David or the Branch of Jesse. The question of who is the Lion, is a good one considering that King Solomon is King David's son and both are descendants of Jesse. (For a good listing of the lineages see the Gospel of Luke.)

The answer is found in the Volume of the Sacred Law in Revelation Chapter 22 verse 16: (NIRV) "I, Jesus, have sent my angel to give you this witness for the churches. I am the Root and the Son of David. I am the bright Morning Star." (It reads pretty much the same way in all 30 translations that I have.)

This is only one explanation of the Lion of the Tribe of Judah. It happens to be the only one I am familiar with or have found in all the research I have done both Masonically and scripturally. I hope this helps to inspire you to find out for yourself what you can glean from the ritual and compare it to your Volume of the Sacred Law no matter what that may be.

If this stirs you to debate and research this subject and starts you down a path of discovery, then I have accomplished the task I set out to do. If it confirms a belief that you already possess then maybe, I have in some small way I have provided the substantiation and helped give you a foundation for your belief. If all you derive after reading this is "ehhh", then I have failed and for that I am sorry.

Masonry is full of discovery and questions. It is a path whose journey is life long and as exciting as you want to make it. Take full advantage of the knowledge of "older and wiser" brethren to "Help you make a greater difference."

CHAPTER 15
WHO WROTE THIS STUFF?

"The guy who wrote this lecture must have been smoking something. It is the most tongue twisting thing I have ever read. You really want me to memorize this?" Jack Rodale inquired of his district lecturer. "When was this written?"

"Yes, I would like for you to memorize it. You do a beautiful job on the ritual you do know. But knowing the why could help you in your decision." Replied the wise lecturer knowing it would excite his curiosity.

Jack Rodale had been a Mason for a little over three years and had become very proficient in many of the ritual parts. He has started through the advancing line of his lodge currently as Junior Deacon and knows the Stewards and Senior Deacon's parts in the initiation as well as his own. His thirst for knowledge grew in proportion to his ritual prowess.

Jack, excited by the challenge of the lecturer, started on the long journey of discovering how our lectures in Missouri came into being since being challenged to learn one of them. During his research the name of William Preston kept cropping up. Researching back into the archives of the Masonic Service Association he found a Short Talk bulletin, Volume 12 January 1934 No.1, which explained that four primary American sources of ritual contributed in one way or another to all American Grand Jurisdictions. In part at least, each received their "work"; from The Mother Grand Lodge ritual (1717 to 1753) which was not the ritual of the United Grand Lodge that came into existence in 1813. When the two parts of the original Mother Grand Lodge ("Ancients" and "Moderns") came together, the United Grand Lodge, or Grand Lodge of Reconciliation, formed its ritual from the best of the divergent rituals of the "Ancients" and the "Moderns."

He saw where Missouri derived its ritual from Pennsylvania and Tennessee, which represented the fusion of Pennsylvania and the "Modern Masonry" of North Carolina. In the Baltimore Masonic Convention of 1843, the conclusions of which were adopted in whole or in part by several American Grand Jurisdictions and the work of Rob Morris along with his conservators in which, despite its chilly reception by many Grand Jurisdictions, undoubtedly left its impression on the Missouri Ritual. But who was this William Preston that was popping up in Masonic ritual history? And why was he so important?

Jack's desire for Masonic education was beginning to be expanded beyond his reasoning. While digging deep within the archival library of the Scottish Rite, he found an 1812 edition of William Preston's "Illustrations of Masonry." The table of contents referred to earlier editions which started in 1772 and showed that there are over nine editions to this work. This fact tickled his mind and gave him an enlightening find that started him on a ritual journey into why William Preston's writings are so important to the ritual as we know it. So now, he emotionally commits to spending more time than just reading a lecture.

He started to read an enlightening biography which began with the birth of William Preston on August 7, 1742 in Edinburgh,

Scotland. Preston's father was a law agent which is peculiar to Scotland called a "Writer to the Signet" which enabled him to be eligible to sit on the bench. This gave William an advantage growing up and he entered high school at the early age of six years old.

Jack discovered that Preston withdrew from college after the death of his father and became the secretary to Thomas Ruddiman, who was a celebrated and a well-known linguist. Ruddiman's eyesight made it necessary for Preston to do much of the research work required for Ruddiman's studies in classical and linguistic endeavors. Preston became a printer in Walter Ruddiman's (a brother to Thomas) shop and who he had formerly apprenticed with early in his career.

Jack also noted Preston's desire to follow his literary ability included a move to London in 1760 where he secured a position with William Stranhan, the King's Printer. He stayed in this position for many years serving not only William but his son as well.

Preston, like Jack, had an unquenchable thirst for knowledge. Consequently, after his twelve-hour workday, he enriched his education by further studies. Literary men would call upon Preston for assistance and his advice. These men, as a show of gratitude and acceptance of his literary talent gave him autographed copies of their works. The copies were from authors like Gibbon, Hume, Robertson, and Blair along with many others. In some respects, Jack was envious of the library Preston had acquired but knew that a good Masonic library would contain similar volumes.

Although Jack knew the date and time of his initiation, he was intrigued by the fact that Masonically, Preston's date of initiation was not known. It is believed to be in London some time in 1762 or early 1763. The United Grand Lodge of England (UGLE) has evidence that Preston's Mother Lodge was the lodge meeting at the White Hart Tavern in Strand. This lodge was formed by several Edinburgh Masons on sabbatical in London. They were refused a charter from the Grand Lodge of Scotland; so the Ancients of the Grand Lodge of London granted dispensation to these brethren on March 2, 1763 who claimed that the second person initiated into their lodge was William Preston. The minutes of Athol (ancient) Grand Lodge show that Lodge # 111 was constituted on April 20, 1763 and Preston's name was listed as the twelfth on a roster listing twenty-two members on the charter.

Preston's lodge was re-constituted as Caledonian Lodge No. 325 by Lord Blayney, then Grand Master on November 15th, 1764. This lodge is still known and active in the UGLE as Number 134. This was important to note because according to historians, the presence of some of the most distinguished and prominent Masons of the day were members of the lodge. As Jack Rodale learned, this spurred Preston to make a serious study of Freemasonry.

When Jack started looking through Preston's Illustrations of Masonry, he found this quote from Preston, "When I first had the honor to be elected Master of a lodge, I thought it proper to inform myself fully of the general rules of the Society, that I might be able to fulfill my own duty and officially enforce obedience in others. The methods which I adopted with this view excited in some of superficial knowledge an absolute dislike of what they considered innovations; and in others who were better informed, a jealously of preeminence, which the principles of Masonry ought to have checked."

Jack could see that Preston was engaged in extensive correspondence with Masons from all over the world at that time and found evidence in the UGLE records that Preston had served the Grand Lodge as a Hall Committee member and eventually as the Deputy Grand Secretary under James Heseline. This appointment afforded him an opportunity to acquire the background information needed for what would become Illustrations of Masonry.

Studying the life of Preston confirmed what Jack had thought all along: that extending one's education in Masonry is only accomplished by diligent work and burning the so-called mid-night oil. Jack learned that Preston also found a vast body of traditional and historical lore in the old documents of the Craft and seized the opportunity of modernizing the ritual in such a way as to make accessible a rudimentary knowledge of the arts and sciences to the members of the Fraternity.

With the approval of the leading members of the Craft, Preston had taken the old lectures and work of Freemasonry, revised them, and placed them in such a form as to fit the modern language of the time. Jack was shocked to learn that Preston had, with his own money, paid lecturers to travel throughout the kingdom and place the lectures before the lodges. Also new editions of his book were demanded by the lodges and thus it was also printed in several European languages.

Jack concluded that Preston's journey through the craft was not without tenuous problems but that the effort and the chronicles which he left behind became the guiding influence of Masonic ritual. That influence is still felt and said every day in every lodge in Missouri when we give a candidate the lecture of a particular degree. For without Preston's original Illustrations we might not have the lectures of the three degrees. It was at the Baltimore conference in 1843 that most Grand Lodge jurisdictions in the US adopted Preston's lectures with minor revisions to fit the US Grand Lodges.

Jack returned to lodge one night and gave his report to the entire body of members present. He concluded his Masonic Education by stating, "It was William Preston who first contributed the Masonic lectures we use today." After it was all said and done his district lecturer still asked, "Well are you going to learn the lecture or not?"

Authors note; I have witnessed the lectures in quite a few Grand Lodge jurisdictions, and it is remarkable that the lectures and the charges are almost word for word identical while the ritual of the actual degree can be so different. For further information on William Preston, consult "Illustrations of Masonry" by William Preston, Pietre-Stones Review of Freemasonry, Wikipedia, and the United Grand Lodge of England.

CHAPTER 16
BOAZ AND JACHIN

The Masonic education I have for you will be in a little different format that what most are used to hearing. It will be from the Great Light of Masonry.

How many of you remember what the Senior Deacon's lecture in the 2nd degree talked about? The first part of that lecture talks about the pillars in the front porch of King Solomon's Temple. I am not sure why we call it King Solomon's Temple because he built it for the Lord and it was dedicated as the Temple of the Lord.

From recent research, we call it King Solomon's Temple because it was Solomon that was charged by God to build the temple. Our Masonic legends, not only in Blue Lodge, but in the Scottish Rite and the York Rite, use the construction of the temple as the cornerstone of some of the degrees. The legend was derived from the Biblical people mentioned in Kings and Numbers as having a major part in the construction of the temple.

The two pillars of the temple were located at the entrance of the temple. As we look at the entrance, these two pillars were massive. They were cast of molten Bronze and adorned with network, lily work and pomegranates. The networking was, and is, a symbol of which signifies unity; the lily work from the whiteness of the lily and the position in which it grows is symbolic of peace; and the pomegranates because of its seeds denotes plenty.

These pillars were 35 cubits in height, 12 cubits in circumference or 4 cubits in diameter. This equates to approximately 53 feet high, 18 feet in circumference or 6 feet in diameter. Keep in mind that the Chapiters, or ornamental tops to the pillars, were another 5 cubits in height or another 8 feet. In the book of 1 Kings 7, the description of the pillars is given. We do not know how big the globes were, but we can assume they were in proportion to the size of the pillars as a whole which we can come to the conclusion that the pillars were approximately 75 feet tall in total.

As we look at the entrance to the temple, the pillar on the left was called Boaz. His story is found in the book of Ruth. 2 Chronicles 2:10-13, Matthew 1:5 and Luke 3:32 which gives us the lineage of Boaz and shows that he is the Great Grandfather of King David or King Solomon's Great Great Grandfather. His name in the ancient Hebrew means "Strength".

The pillar on the right was called Jachin. We have a discrepancy between versions of the Bible as to how it was spelled. Some of the newer versions show it being spelled as JAKIN. But, the ritual and literal Hebrew spelling is as we use it with a CH. instead of a K. Jachin is a personal name and means "YAH Established" or "God Established". He is the 4th Son of Simeon and original ancestor of a clan in the tribe which is denoted as Jarib in 1 Chronicles 4:24. He is a priest who lived in Nehemiah's time and is from Jerusalem. In the listing of priests as found in 1 Chronicles 9:10 and Nehemiah 11:10 we find that he is the 21st priest in the rotation of priests to care for the temple or as the Hebrews call it "ministering to the House of the Lord". Nehemiah chapters 9, 10 and 11 show the order of Priesthood and who was assigned to do what and how many it took.

King Solomon in his wisdom, according to several commentaries, used these two individuals to name the pillars in keeping with the prophecy which states, "In Strength, will I Establish thy house forever". Many theologians conclude and agree this prophecy refers to the coming reign of the Messiah and his kingdom. Freemasonry does not speculate on this aspect of the prophecy but uses it as a literal description of the temple only and the meaning behind the two pillars.

Freemasonry lore also supposes that Hiram Abif cast and built the pillars. There is no concrete evidence to support the claim, but the inference and conclusion can be made to support this. Hiram Abif actually spelled Hirum, in some of the translations, is mentioned very few times and there seems to be some confusion as to whether it is the same person. What we do know is that Hiram Abif, as described in 1 Kings 7:13, was a skilled craftsman in the art of metals, stone, wood and colors of fabric and fine linens. He was a master engraver and designer according to the writings of Josephus. His mother was a widow from the tribe of Naphtali and his father was from the kingdom of Tyre which explains his knowledge in the craft arts. According to Josephus, the Jewish historian, and Esubious, a Roman historian, we know that Hiram Abif did complete the temple and was commissioned to build other buildings for King Herod before his death.

The columns which you see on the warden's pedestals are representative of these two main pillars. The junior Warden's pillar represents Boaz and the Senior Warden's column is a representation of Jachin. Historical writings from the Cathedral Era of Europe show that the craft guilds of England and Europe established them as a means of distinguishing when the paymaster of wages was in his office. Early writings denote that, who we now call the Senior Warden, was in fact in charge of the construction and pay for the workmen. The Junior Warden was the person in charge of all the lodging, food and drink for the workmen during mealtimes and after the work day was completed. Hence the explanation of why we change the position of the columns at certain times of the ritual.

The main lessons of Boaz and Jachin are found within the decorative elements themselves. Brother Kevin Hampton from Kearney Lodge #311 made this observation, "Also in relation to these 2 pillars as representing parallels of mankind, we should study the illustration of their ornamental adornments. The lily, and the retired situation in which it flourishes, teaches us that we must learn to open our minds and hearts to all of mankind; to retain the fact, in our compassion, that as one pillar only serves to support the other, we are also obligated, and should offer our support, not only to the brother who may have stumbled and fell by the wayside of life but to the aggregate of all mankind; to offer help, aid and assistance to those who may be in need; and to make that total concentrated effort to add to and not subtract from, the whole of human existence."

Brother Hampton also defines the network in this manner, "From the intricate connection of the network, we can also perceive that all of mankind must learn to live in peace and harmony with his brothers, sisters and with nature; to appreciate the beauties which the Great Architect of the Universe has given to us to enjoy and not to dominate, exploit, or manipulate it; and finally we should be taught to discern the sounds of Brotherly Love which ring loud and true to all those who will only take the time to listen."

In concluding the explanation of the elements Brother Hampton states, "The pomegranates and their exuberance of seeds proclaim to too many in their minds, seeds of skepticism. To the avaricious person that vast number of seeds represents Greed and its collaboration, the selfishness of despotism, because the word Charity and the symbolic intention of this fruit is alien and anonymous to them. To the enlightened and true man, who practices the application of his Masonic teachings, these pomegranates manifest the plenty which our Great Architect of the Universe has provided for all. It is individuals of this caliber who have come to understand the true meaning of the pillar's adornments; men whom unquestionably enjoy sharing the bounties of life and that the abundances of our earth were placed here to be apportioned equally."

The two pommels or globes, the meaning of which, as described in the ritual, is to encourage the study of the sciences and does not have an alternate meaning other than to allude to the first-degree lecture which announces to the whole of humanity that Masonry is as unending and as universal as the blue arch of heaven.

My brothers, we may conclude from the Bible, the ritual, the explanations of the symbols and Brother Hampton's observations that the most inspiring feature of these two pillars is the fact that they were created to be of equal status and as such we were certainly given the power to be our brother's keeper, to console with our brother in his time of need and to share with him in times when the joys of life abound.

In closing, stop and ponder the lessons taught by these two pillars which are on guard at the entrance of our lodge room.

As these are on guard, as silent sentinels to our work, so should we ever see them as the entrance and pathway for all men to walk in Charity, Relief and Brotherly Love.

CHAPTER 17

WHY ARE SO MANY MASONS BORED WITH THE BIBLE?

"Unfortunately, many Christians love the idea of the Bible, but not really the Bible itself."

We love having a Bible close by, even within reach, but don't make time to open it on an average day. We talk about Bible reading like we talk about cutting calories or cleaning our house. We're grateful for the results, but we don't wake up dying to do it again. It sounds like a fine thing to do, until we have to choose what we won't do in order to make time for it.

If that's you, you probably also know a Christian who loves reading their Bible. They can't get enough of it. As far as you know, they would just as likely go a whole day without food as without the Bible. Their happy discipline convicts and, if you're honest, sometimes even annoys you. Who is it in your life who is most likely to pray like this?

"I enjoy reading the Bible more than the wealthy enjoy all their houses, cars, technology and vacations. God, your word will be my first priority and focus each day. I will read and read the Bible, until I cannot forget it. Give me more grace, O God, and enable me to obey what I've read. Help me see more today than I've already seen before, even in these same pages. I only wish I had more time to read more of my Bible."

Does that sound like you? Or more likely someone you know? Do you feel at home in a love like that? Or have you delegated that kind of personality and affection to other "more spiritual" people?

God, Open Our Eyes and Hearts

The prayer above is a paraphrase of a prayer in Psalm 119:14–20:

In the way of your testimonies I delight as much as in all riches. I will meditate on your precepts and fix my eyes on your ways. I will delight in your statutes; I will not forget your word. Deal bountifully with your servant, that I may live and keep your word. Open my eyes, that I may behold wondrous things out of your law. I am a sojourner on the earth; hide not your commandments from me! My soul is consumed with longing for your rules at all times.

Reading a prayer like that usually levels me. The psalmist's passionate love for God's word can make me uncomfortable. The love seems so real, so right, so beautiful—and so foreign, at least some days. Why do I wake up worried about what's on Twitter, Instagram or Facebook, instead of wanting to open the Bible? Why am I more excited to read the best new book on whatever, rather than the only book with the very words of God? Why am I still likely to find my identity and worth in what I have or what I've done, instead of what God says about me? Why am I bored reading the Bible while the psalmist is having the time of his life?

He says, "It is good for me that I was afflicted, that I might learn your statutes" (Psalm 119:71). The author praises God for pain, because he believes the pain helped him understand God and his word better. Have you ever been able to draw a line like that, between your suffering and your Bible reading? He goes on, "The law of your mouth is better to me than thousands of gold and silver pieces" (Psalm 119:72). What if you had to pay five dollars every time you read your Bible? What would your Bible budget be this month?

So why Are We Bored?

A lot of us want to relegate love like this to others. Some people love the Bible, and some people love people. Or, some people like to read, and some people like to serve. But the Bible, like the gospel, can't be relegated only to a few. Bible reading isn't a spiritual gift like Bible teaching, or biblical counseling, or speaking in tongues. Bible reading and loving is a gift (and calling) for all believers.

Psalm 119 does not model extraordinary Christianity. It's showing us how people truly in love with God receive actual words from God. They realize the awesome gift they've received in this book. When they open their Bibles, or hear the Bible read or preached, they can feel as though God himself were walking down from heaven to speak to them.

I admit I have a hard time remembering and feeling that some mornings. Why are so many Christians bored with the Bible? Because we've forgotten what the Bible is.

John Piper reminds us, again, narrating his personal Bible reading with wonder,

"Think of it. Marvel at this. Stand in awe of this. The God who keeps watch over the nations, like some people keep watch over cattle or stock markets or construction sites—this God still speaks in the 21st century.... By this voice, he speaks with absolute truth and personal force. By this voice, he reveals his all-surpassing beauty. By this voice, he reveals the deepest secrets of our hearts. No voice anywhere anytime can reach as deep or lift as high or carry as far as the voice of God that we hear in the Bible."

Absolute truth. Personal power and relevance. All-surpassing beauty. All-knowing love and wisdom. All from the mind and mouth of God. All in the pages of a book we can hold in one hand.

CHAPTER 18

IN THE BEGINNING GOD...

When we knelt at the altar for our first obligation and upon calming down, listening to the master of the lodge; we heard these words:

"In the beginning God created the heavens and the earth. Now the earth was formless and empty, darkness was over the surface of the deep, and the Spirit of God was hovering over the waters. And God said, 'Let there be light,' and there was light. God saw that the light was good, and he separated the light from the darkness. God called the light 'day,' and the darkness he called 'night.' And there was evening, and there was morning—the first day" (Genesis 1:1-5, NIV).

When you joined the lodge was it your first time in a group of people, what character or good quality of yours that you would like first to project or promote? Or, what is your particular character that you would like others to notice at once?

Is it your physical appearance?

Just your simplicity?

Now, how did God present Himself in the very beginning?

So, this time, let us try what we could also …. KNOW GOD IN THE BEGINNING… as we deal with this lesson from the First Degree of Masonry (Genesis 1:1-5).

Again, what do you think God would like us to know about Him in the very beginning?

The book of Genesis is not an ordinary historical narrative. Modern histories focus only on the activities of the people, but the book includes within its scope the activities of God.

Genesis, as included in the first five books of the Bible, known as the Pentateuch, was unanimously believed both by Christians and Jews that it was compiled and written by Moses. He wrote it in the Wilderness of Sinai about 15th century BC.

"…Moses wrote and compiled Genesis to encourage the early Israelites while they were preparing to enter the land of Canaan, the Promised Land. The content of Genesis would have been especially significant to them…" Would you agree that in the initial verses of the Book, Moses may be trying to remind them just Who is this God, and who will bring them to their destination.

In lodge the signposts of who God is are all over. Those of us who, in our time, received the promise that we will be in His Kingdom, ought to really know and remember the same God, who brought the Israelites triumphantly in the promised land.

So, what could we learn about God in the opening words of the Scripture?

First, He is the Eternal Creator (verses 1-2).

We read in verses 1-2, "In the beginning God created the heavens and the earth. Now the earth was formless and empty, darkness was over the surface of the deep, and the Spirit of God was hovering over the waters."

Notice the first few words, "In the beginning God..." The author never hinted that he would attempt to prove the existence of God. Rather, he declared without any hesitation that there is God. In your initial investigation before the lodge approved you for membership, you too had to believe there is a God. So therefore, in Masonry, like Moses said, "In the Beginning God..."

And if we will make a word study of the word "beginning," we'll realize that in the transliteration of the Hebrew "reshith" – it is not limited in the meaning of "beginning," but could also be translated, "chief," "choice part," "absolute chief thing," etc. Thus, instead of questioning the existence of God, we need to realize that He is the main thing. But considering the common understanding of the word beginning in the text, the passage does not declare that is He just the Creator. He is the Eternal Creator. "Eternal" does not just mean, "everlasting," but also "having no beginning and no end." "In the beginning God..." the author indicated "that at the beginning of recorded time, God was already in existence. From duration stretching backward without limit to duration stretching forward without limit, from eternal ages to eternal ages, God was and is forever."

As we knelt at the altar during those first few moments, we need to consider that Masonically we have been created in darkness. Not that there wasn't light in the room, or from the altar lights, but from a knowledge viewpoint, that we were dark in the knowledge of masonry and that knowledge was about to become enlightened knowledge.

Let's continue to read the passage, "...God created the heavens and the earth. Now the earth was formless and empty, darkness was over the surface of the deep, and the Spirit of God was hovering over the waters." It is also noteworthy that this this Eternal Creator was introduced as an Active God. He was not presented as an Eternal God who is just sitting, resting, lying down, or doing nothing. He is at work. In fact, He creates, He is hovering, He is really on the move.

We as Masons have a tendency of to brush aside this eternal creative power of God. We may take it lightly, but God does not. We read in Romans 1:18 a reminder of the lesson we should heed as Masons.

"The wrath of God is being revealed from heaven against all the godlessness and wickedness of people, who suppress the truth by their wickedness..." What is this suppression? Let's proceed to verses 19-21: "... since what may be known about God is plain to them, because God has made it plain to them. For since the creation of the world God's invisible qualities — his eternal power and divine nature — have been clearly seen, being understood from what has been made, so that people are without excuse. For although they knew God, they neither glorified him as God nor gave thanks to him, but their thinking became futile and their foolish hearts were darkened."

God's existence is evident. As not only quoted by Moses but reinforced in Romans. His Eternal Creative Power is evident. So, Masons are without excuse. Yet, they suppress that truth in their mind and manufactured a kind of god that serve their selfish purpose. Yes, that statement can be a little harsh, but at the heart of all religions, in one form or another is God. What mankind has done over time is to cloud that fact. How about us, saints, Masons, and believers do we acknowledge the intense Majesty of God, as Eternal Creator by glorifying Him not just by words, but also by our works? Do we always thank Him, not only by the events He is creating in our life, but also for Who He is?

As we learn from our Rituals, do we really believe that He is the Glorious God? I am in no way stating that our rituals replace the Great Light of Masonry. What I am saying is that contained within our rituals are the lessons from the Great Light and that this one is one of the first and major lessons we should learn. May no Mason just believe it and yet think or behave as if he – not God -- is the one who deserves the glory, the attention, the favor, or every good thing from others.

What else could we learn about God in our passage during this point of the ceremony?

Well, He is the Supreme Personal Being (verses 3-4A). I used the term Personal Being for a reason. He is not an ordinary person. He speaks. He sees or evaluates and determines what is good. We further read in verses 3-4A, "And God said, 'Let there be light,' and there was light. God saw that the light was good, ..." God is not a just a "thing." He is not just an idea or principle. When He speaks, it comes into being.

Father said, "Let there be light," light became a reality, though the physical source of it was created during the fourth day. It is at this point our rituals and Masonic meanings become a little clearer. There have been explanations presented why light was mentioned here in first day of creation, though the sun and other sources of light created only during the fourth day, Masonically it happened on your first day as a Mason. If you remember that part of your ceremony, the wording was something like, "in humble commemoration of that august event..." We brought you to light in Masonic knowledge. Gave you the light to see the Great Light of Masonry and learn its lessons as God has given us light to see creation and learn the lessons, he has placed there for us to learn.

There is but another lesson we overlook both spiritually and Masonically. We have a Supreme Personal Being, who is Eternal, and who is the Great Architect of the Universe. Sometimes we fail to realize that if there was no sun or moon, light could happen for He Himself is Light.

We also learn that He is not an ordinary Personal Being. Just because what He speaks becomes a reality, but what comes from Him, which is the result of His creative action, is really good. In fact, because of it, not only does it show that He is truly a good personal being, but He Himself is the standard of what is really good. If Masons, as well as all of us, have the tendency to set aside the eternal power of God, it becomes clear that it is even farther from their minds to entertain that God is the supreme personal being, who is really good. This leads us to the question are we inclined to question the goodness of God?

The situation is, we even prefer to cling to the worldly standard of goodness. And what is sad is that sometimes we embrace the good relationship that we have from other human beings over the relationship we could have with the Father. As Masons, saints or true believers, we must ask ourselves, "Do we truly regard God as the

Supreme Personal Being, or do we really value the opportunity that we could have a relationship with Him, because He is also a personal being?" When we realize that He is supremely good and loving as well, do we seek to develop a closer relationship with Him?

In discussing this with other Masonic pastors, the following questions arose as a result of the lessons learned in this brief discussion. Do we love to spend our time with Him? Do we desire to come to praise and worship Him? Do we always talk to Him in prayer? Do we pray to Him when we are just in need, or are we also excited to share our joys and gratitude to Him? Our rituals and public ceremonies are riddled with prayers, requests and praises to our Heavenly Father. Sometimes we focus more on the words instead of learning the meaning behind the words and the lesson of those words.

Finally, my brethren – and ladies too, are we always eager to listen to His Words? Shouldn't we invest more time in reading, studying, meditating, listening to His Word. We do this with our ritual which contains the lessons from the Great Light why not study the Great Light right along with our rituals? As a supreme personal God, His words have power effect. Remember also Isaiah 55:10-11:

"As the rain and the snow come down from heaven, and do not return to it without watering the earth and making it bud and flourish, so that it yields seed for the sower and bread for the eater, so is my word that goes out from my mouth: It will not return to me empty, but will accomplish what I desire and achieve the purpose for which I sent it."

If we read past that point ritualistically that applies to these verses and finish the paragraph so to speak, we could also learn that, He is

Sovereign (verses 4B-5). "... and he separated the light from the darkness. God called the light 'day,' and the darkness he called 'night.' And there was evening, and there was morning—the first day."

God is not just a Creator; He is Sovereign. He is in absolute control of what He created. When He created the light, He separated it from the darkness. When He called or named the light "day," and the darkness "night," it proves that He is a ruler, in control, of the universe.

The naming of these elements of creation is a mark of God's sovereignty. In the thinking of the peoples of the ancient Middle East, naming something was a mark of power or lordship. For them, names were not merely labels, but descriptions with some force to them.

God is truly Sovereign, in control, of not only His inanimate creation, but also in the events of the world and the affairs of men. In the New Living Translation, we read Proverbs 21:1, "The king's heart is like a stream of water directed by the LORD; he guides it wherever he pleases."

Notice that not just the heart of an ordinary man, but even of a sovereign human ruler – his desire or will is directed by God. Now, in the NIV we read Proverbs 19:9, "In their hearts humans plan their course, but the LORD establishes their steps." And in Provers 21:30-31, "There is no wisdom, no insight, no plan that can succeed against the LORD. The horse is made ready for the day of battle, but victory rests with the LORD." We plan, we can prepare, of which it is our human responsibility to do so, but the result is in the Hands of the Sovereign God.

How about us Masons, do we acknowledge God's Sovereignty over our lives? Or, are we influenced by the other practices in the world which pressure us to believe that on own ability, we can chart our own destiny? And because of it do we tend to manipulate others to fulfill what we want to achieve in life, or do we help them to achieve what they want to accomplish as well?

Or, as in some cases, are we on the other extreme, do we refrain to plan and prepare and just erroneously assume that God will make all things happen for us? I know I fall into that category and some will fall in that error. We must not fail to acknowledge that the means by which those plans are to succeed are also determined by God, not just the result.

Brethren, in spite of our best efforts and a well-prepared plan, if the result is not what we desire, we can still find comfort in the knowledge that our God is Sovereign. He is in control of all things whether we realize it or not. "And we know that in all things God works for the good of those who love him, who have been called according to his purpose." (Romans 8:28)

To summarize our experience at the altar in being brought to Masonic Light for the first time, we have seen that God is an eternal creator, that He is a supreme personal God and He is sovereign. However, sometimes this is not enough. The unbelievers know it, but they suppress it. The devil knows it and he hates it.

But will we really love to know that God is Eternal Creator, He is the Supreme Personal Being and He is Sovereign. Will we love him enough to see the Lion of the tribe of Judah? Will we really delight in that Truth, because we are given the right to become His children? He is now our Father, who is the Eternal Creator, Supreme Personal Being and Sovereign in control of all things.

CHAPTER 19
WHY DID YOUR MAN JOIN THE MASONS?

It was 10:30 as Lauren was snuggled deep within the covers of the bed reading her latest book when she heard her husband of 10 years come through the door. Mike, an aspiring career minded individual, made his way as quietly as possible to the bedroom. Lauren looked inquisitively at him and asked, "Well, how did it go?"

"Fine." Mike responded.

"What happened?" she asked.

"I can't tell you." He responded. Knowing that it was going to cause a barrage of questions of which he neither had the answers for and if he did he still couldn't tell her.

"What do you mean you can't tell me? We have been totally open and honest with each other and share everything. I don't understand why you can't tell me what happened. It just doesn't make sense."

Honey, I'm sorry. I just can't. I was told I couldn't share the ceremonies with anyone including my wife."

Well, if that's the way you're going to be, then good night." With that she turned out the light, rolled over and gave that sigh that only wives can give when we are in deep trouble.

Mike laid there thinking about what had transpired that night, trying to remember what was said, what he had seen and the people he had met. He didn't remember much, but he felt a twinge of excitement from the experience.

Sound familiar? Sometimes these conversations carry a different connotation. Sometimes the wife understands upfront that she will not be able to find out anything. Sometimes her past family members have told her "It's a guy thing" and not to even ask questions; especially if there were any Masons in the family. This doesn't cure her curiosity; it only adds fuel to the fire.

So what started this process? Let's look back a couple of months ago when Mike came home from work and make that famous announcement.

"Honey, guess what? I'm going to be a Mason and a Shriner and it's only going to cost me a couple of hundred dollars."

"Great. You're going to spend money we don't have to join a group I don't know anything about and be gone from the kids who need you're support in their activities. What is a Mason?"

His response is usually, "I don't know. I got to join them to be a Shriner. You know the guys with the funny red hats and do the circus thing once a year and have those hospitals."

Sometimes the wife's response centers around questions like, "You're going to join a bunch of drunks on motorcycles and ride around with that goofy hat on your head and embarrass us?" or "Why in God's name would you want to join that?"

Ladies, in all honesty, at that time he usually has no clue. All he knew at the time was his friends and acquaintances were joining and it seemed like fun at the time. What he was really thinking was, "I get to be a kid again and it's legal."

However, on the other side of the spectrum lies the fact that he sought out someone to become a Mason because his father or grandfather was a member and he understood and believed that his father and grandfather were great men and wanted to be like them. Most of the time they join because of their grandfather. Men have a great affection for their grandfathers and want to be just like them in most cases.

Another reason men join the fraternity is because their father-in-law is a member and he wants to keep peace in the family. Get his father-in-law off his back so to speak. Some men join because they were in DeMolay as a youth and it is a natural progression for them to become Masons. Still, others have heard something about the Fraternity whether good or bad and wanted to check it out. A good percentage of the men joining the Fraternity today is that the wives are members of the Order of the Eastern Star and they are encouraging their husbands to join the Masons so they attend Star with them or at least have a deeper understanding of what the Fraternity is and thus have another common bond in their marriage.

But the number one reason I hear the most centers on a family member that was a Mason. When I inquire as to why he waited so long to join the reply usually is: "No one asked me until now." For you guys, that is a big hint on what you need to do. The number two reason I hear is that they have always wanted to join but decided to wait until the kids were grown up, in college or married and they felt they finally had enough time to devout to the lodge. We see this in baby boomers.

Today we are seeing two major groups of men joining the Fraternity. We see the Boomers, ages 45 to 60 and the younger men ages of 21 to 30. That 10 to 15-year gap is the guys with families and careers who are afraid to devout the time required to attend meetings once or twice a month.

Now let's jump ahead a few years, was it worth it ladies? Did you see the small changes over time in his behavior, in his attitude, in his maturity in certain areas?

In his progression through the three degrees he learned that he could not divulge any of the secrets of freemasonry to anyone who was not a member. That's what started the attitude when he came home that first night. When he got his second degree, he learned that he was to contribute to the relief of distressed worthy brothers.

His maturity level will increase as he learns valuable lessons in dealing with people as he progresses through the officer line. The lessons taught in our ritual have planted the seeds of being a man with virtue, integrity and honor to all people.

Your man learns Psalm 133 which exemplifies that how good and how pleasant is for us to dwell together in unity. He learns a deeper meaning and a better understanding of Brotherly Love, Relief and Truth. The Cardinal Virtues of Temperance, Fortitude, Prudence and Justice bring on a new and added dimension to his life.

The seed of betterment from the Worshipful Master's charge at the closing of the meeting begins to add a new dimension to his life and character.

Brethren, you are now to quit this sacred retreat of friendship and virtue to mix again with the world. Amidst its concerns and employments forget not the duties that you have heard so frequently inculcated and forcibly recommended in this lodge. Remember that around this alter you have promised to befriend and relieve every worthy brother who shall need your assistance. Remember that you have promised to remind him in the most tender manner of his failings and aid his reformation. These generous principles are to extend further. Every human being has a claim upon your kind offices; do good unto all, recommend it more especially to the house hold of the faithful and finally Brethren, be ye all of one mind live in peace and may the God of love and peace delight to dwell with and bless you.

But more importantly in his third degree he learns that the contributions to distressed worthy brothers includes the wives, widows and orphans of those brothers. He took an obligation which binds him to be faithful to his wife and to honor and respect the wives, widows, mothers, sisters and daughters of Master Masons.

Although not directly in our ritual, but through the meaning of the symbols and emblems we use, he learns in Proverbs 31 verses 10 through 31 the following:

A wife of noble character who can find?
She is worth far more than rubies.

Her husband has full confidence in her
and lacks nothing of value.
She brings him good, not harm,
all the days of her life.
She selects wool and flax
and works with eager hands.
She is like the merchant ships,
bringing her food from afar.
She gets up while it is still dark;
she provides food for her family
and portions for her servant girls.
She considers a field and buys it;
out of her earnings she plants a vineyard.
She sets about her work vigorously;
her arms are strong for her tasks.
She sees that her trading is profitable,
and her lamp does not go out at night.
In her hand she holds the distaff
and grasps the spindle with her fingers.
She opens her arms to the poor
and extends her hands to the needy.
When it snows, she has no fear for her household;

for all of them are clothed in scarlet.

She makes coverings for her bed;

she is clothed in fine linen and purple.

Her husband is respected at the city gate,

where he takes his seat among the elders of the land.

She makes linen garments and sells them,

and supplies the merchants with sashes.

She is clothed with strength and dignity;

she can laugh at the days to come.

She speaks with wisdom,

and faithful instruction is on her tongue.

She watches over the affairs of her household

and does not eat the bread of idleness.

Her children arise and call her blessed;

her husband also, and he praises her:

Many women do noble things,

but you surpass them all."

Charm is deceptive, and beauty is fleeting;

but a woman who fears the LORD is to be praised.

Give her the reward she has earned,

and let her works bring her praise at the city

These words that are only a small token of our appreciation as husbands and Masons. It is our way of saying thank you for allowing us to attend the meetings and to re-affirm our love and devotion to you and for the sacrifices you have made for us.

Ladies, I hope you find and have found whether it is worth it for your husband to be a member of this great an honorable fraternity and carry the title of Master Mason.

CHAPTER 20

SACRIFICES

After a few of the usual Sunday evening hymns, the church's pastor slowly stood up, walked over to the pulpit and, before he gave his sermon for the evening, briefly introduced a guest minister who was in the service that evening. In the introduction, the pastor told the congregation that the guest minister was one of his dearest friends and that he wanted him to have a few moments to greet the church and share whatever he felt would be appropriate for the service. With that, an elderly man stepped up to the pulpit and began to speak, "A father, his son, and a friend of his son were sailing off the Pacific Coast," he began, "when a fast approaching storm blocked any attempt to get back to shore. The waves were so high, that even though the father was an experienced sailor, he could not keep the boat upright, and the three were swept into the ocean as the boat capsized."

The old man hesitated for a moment, making eye contact with two teenagers who were, for the first time since the service began, looking somewhat interested in his story. The aged minister continued with "Grabbing a rescue line, the father had to make the most excruciating decision of his life to which boy he would throw the other end of the lifeline. He only had seconds to make the decision. The father knew that his son was a Christian and he also knew that his son's friend was not. The agony of his decision could not be matched by the torrent of waves. "As the father yelled out, 'I love you, son!' he threw out the lifeline to his son's friend. By the time the father had pulled the friend back to the capsized boat, his son had disappeared beneath the raging swells into the black of night. His body was never recovered."

By this time, the two teenagers were sitting up straight in the pew, anxiously waiting for the next words to come out of the old minister's mouth. "The father," he continued, "knew his son would step into eternity with Jesus, and he could not bear the thought of his son's friend stepping into an eternity without Jesus. Therefore, he sacrificed his son to save the son's friend. How great is the love of God that He should do the same for us? Our heavenly Father sacrificed His only begotten Son that we could be saved. I urge you to accept His offer to rescue you and take hold of the life line He is throwing out to you in this service." With that, the old man turned and sat back down in his chair as silence filled the room. The pastor again walked slowly to the pulpit and delivered a brief sermon with an invitation at the end. However, no one responded to the appeal.

Within minutes after the service ended, the two teenagers were at the old man's side. "That was a nice story," politely started one of the boys, "but I don't think it was very realistic for a father to give up his only son's life in hopes that the other boy would become a Christian." "Well, you've got a point there," the old man replied, glancing down at his worn Bible. A big smile broadened his narrow face, and he once again looked up at the boys and said, "It sure isn't very realistic, is it? But I'm standing here today to tell you that THAT story gives me a glimpse of what it must have been like for God to give up His Son for me. In it I see the real mercy and grace of God. You see I was that father and your pastor is my son's friend."

Masonry abounds with stories like this and others. Does our ritual contain lessons that we may learn to apply the stories like this? Yes, it does. Examine if you will, the lesson of the third degree. We learn that Abiff sacrificed his life in order to save what? If we look at the story, we see that he gave his life, not unlike Jesus which some have come to conclude, but to save the reputation of the others, to keep his word. We learn from the Volume of Sacred Law or The Great Light in Masonry, that God's word is true, and the God always keeps his word.

Learning the lesson of keeping your word is the hall mark of a Mason. I remember my father telling me, "If a Mason ever gives you his word, it is his bond to you and you can take it to the bank because a mason will always keep his word." Was Dad ever let down by a mason. Yes. Did dad ever give up on the character of masons? No. You see, my father was a mason also and did his best to keep his word even if it meant sacrificing time and money to help someone else. Have you learned those valuable lessons yet?

In our society today, we are too quick to get things in writing to prevent lawsuits. We are too quick to define responsibilities and duties we need to perform in the lodge as well as outside the lodge. Is this a good thing? Sometimes it can be more of a hindrance than a benefit. Where it hurts is that a mason working under this guise, is not keeping his word as a moral obligation but a legal one. That fine line is getting fuzzier as time goes by and we are losing sight of what it means to keep your word.

Did the Old Preacher in the story at the beginning keep his word? Did his son's friend keep his word to his friend's father?

But, more importantly, did his son's friend keep his word to his Lord for saving his life? Food for you to ponder as you continue your Masonic Journey and building your Masonic edifice.

CHAPTER 21

ANCHOR AND ARK

In the third-degree lecture there is a paragraph about an anchor and an ark. Most men assume that the anchor has reference to anchoring our lives to God as taught in the Great Light of Masonry and they would be correct. For we read in Hebrews 6:19a (NIV) "We have this hope as an anchor for the soul, firm and secure. It enters the inner sanctuary behind the curtain,"

Which hope we have as an anchor—The apostle here changes the allusion; he represents the state of the followers of God in this lower world as resembling that of a vessel striving to perform her voyage through a troublesome, tempestuous, dangerous sea. At last she gets near the port; but the tempest continues, the water is shallow, broken, and dangerous, and she cannot get in: in order to prevent her being driven to sea again she heaves out her sheet anchor, which she has been able to get within the pier head by means of her boat, though she could not herself get in; then, swinging at the length of her cable, she rides out the storm in confidence, knowing that her anchor is sound, the ground good in which it is fastened, and the cable strong. Though agitated, she is safe; though buffeted by wind and tide, she does not drive; by and by the storm ceases, the tide flows in, her sailors take to the capstan, wear the ship against the anchor, which still keeps its bite or hold, and she gets safely into port. (Adam Clarke's Commentary on Hebrews 6:19)

The comparison of hope to an anchor is frequent among the ancient writers, who supposed it necessary to the support of a man in adversity, as the anchor is to the safety of the ship when about to be driven on a lee shore by a storm. "To ground hope on a false supposition," says Socrates, "is like trusting to a weak anchor." He said farther, ουτε ναυν εξ ενος αγκυριου, ουτε βιον εκ μιας ελπιδος ὁρμιστεον· a ship ought not to trust to one anchor, nor life to one hope. Stob., Serm. 109.

Adam Clarke's Commentary explains that the hope of an eternal life is represented as the soul's anchor; the world is the wind driven, dangerous sea; the Christian course, the voyage; the port, everlasting life or heaven; and the veil or inner road, the royal dock in which that anchor was cast. We know that the storms of life will continue but a short time; the anchor, hope, if fixed by faith in the eternal world, will infallibly prevent all shipwreck; the soul may/will be strongly tossed by various temptations, but will not slip, because the anchor is in sure ground, and itself is steadfast; it does not drag, and it does not break; faith, like the cable, is the connecting medium between the ship and the anchor, or the soul and its hope of heaven; faith sees the heaven, hope desires and anticipates the rest; faith works, and hope holds fast; and, shortly, the soul enters into the haven of eternal repose.

In masonry we are often asked why we are so at peace. Is it because we are constantly engaged in a personal ministry where our anchor and our ark are safely moored? Or is it because we are constantly spreading the anchor rope through our good deeds and our public service to others?

This reminds me of the story about a man who was asked to paint a boat. He brought his paint and brushes and began to paint the boat a bright red, as the owner asked him. While painting, he noticed a small hole in the hull, and quietly repaired it. When he finished painting, he received his money and left.

The next day, the owner of the boat came to the painter and presented him with a nice check, much higher than the payment for painting. The painter was surprised and said, "You've already paid me for painting the boat Sir!"

"But this is not for the paint job. It's for repairing the hole in the boat."

"Ah! But it was such a small service... certainly it's not worth paying me such a high amount for something so insignificant."

"My dear friend, you do not understand. Let me tell you what happened: When I asked you to paint the boat, I forgot to mention the hole. When the boat dried, my kids took the boat and went on a fishing trip. They did not know that there was a hole. I was not at home at that time. When I returned and noticed they had taken the boat, I was desperate because I remembered that the boat had a hole. Imagine my relief and joy when I saw them returning from fishing. Then, I examined the boat and found that you had repaired the hole! You see, now, what you did? You saved the life of my children! I do not have enough money to pay your 'small' good deed."

So, no matter who, when or how, continue to help, sustain, wipe tears, listen attentively, and carefully repair all the 'leaks' you find. You never know when one is in need of us, or when God holds a pleasant surprise for us to be helpful and important to someone.

Along the way, you may have repaired numerous 'boat holes' for several people without realizing how many lives you've save.

This story is but a small representation of the character and the quality of your character as you learn to ground your hope. It will become evident to others that you are a passenger on that Divine Ark which safely wafts us over this tempestuous sea of troubles and that we are safely moored in in the peaceful harbor. And as such, it has become your responsibility to show others how they too can have a securely anchored hope and become a passenger on the Divine Ark.

CHAPTER 22
How Different Are we?

I watched as the young candidate was escorted into the lodge room. What amazed me was the grumbling I heard from some of the older Past Masters. Grumbling which consisted of phrases like, "In my term we wouldn't have permitted someone like that to be initiated." Or "Why would you want someone like that going through the line?" In all fairness to the old past masters, I understood the sentiment they were so rudely expressing. I knew all too well what they were saying because I have said the same things in the past until I learned a very valuable lesson from Tony, a friend of mine, who chose to love me and correct me instead of criticizing me. Tony's brother is a great human being named Kevin.

Here is the lesson he taught me.

I envy Kevin. My brother, Kevin, thinks God lives under his bed. At least that's what I heard him say one night. He was praying out loud in his dark bedroom, and I stopped to listen, 'Are you there, God?' he said. 'Where are you? Oh, I see. Under the bed....'

I giggled softly and tiptoed off to my own room. Kevin's unique perspectives are often a source of amusement. But that night something else lingered long after the humor. I realized for the first time the very different world Kevin lives in. He was born 30 years ago, mentally disabled as a result of difficulties during labor. Apart from his size (he's 6-foot-2), there are few ways in which he is an adult. He reasons and communicates with the capabilities of a 7-year-old, and he always will. He will probably always believe that God lives under his bed, that Santa Clause is the one who fills the space under our tree every Christmas and that airplanes stay up in the sky because angels carry them.

I remember wondering if Kevin realizes he is different. Is he ever dissatisfied with his monotonous life? Up before dawn each day, off to work at a workshop for the disabled, home to walk our cocker spaniel, return to eat his favorite macaroni-and-cheese for dinner, and later to bed. The only variation in the entire scheme is laundry, when he hovers excitedly over the washing machine like a mother with her newborn child. He does not seem dissatisfied.

He lopes out to the bus every morning at 7:05, eager for a day of simple work. He wrings his hands excitedly while the water boils on the stove before dinner, and he stays up late twice a week to gather our dirty laundry for his next day's laundry chores. And Saturdays - oh, the bliss of Saturdays! That's the day my Dad takes Kevin to the airport to have a soft drink, watch the planes land, and speculate loudly on the destination of each passenger inside. "That one's goin' to Chi-car-go!' Kevin shouts as he claps his hands.

His anticipation is so great he can hardly sleep on Friday nights. And so goes his world of daily rituals and weekend field trips. He doesn't know what it means to be discontent. His life is simple. He will never know the entanglements of wealth of power, and he does not care what brand of clothing he wears or what kind of food he eats. His needs have always been met, and he never worries that one day they may not be.

His hands are diligent. Kevin is never so happy as when he is working. When he unloads the dishwasher or vacuums the carpet, his heart is completely in it. He does not shrink from a job when it is begun, and he does not leave a job until it is finished. But when his tasks are done, Kevin knows how to relax. He is not obsessed with his work or the work of others. His heart is pure. He still believes everyone tells the truth, promises must be kept, and when you are wrong, you apologize instead of argue. Free from pride and unconcerned with appearances, Kevin is not afraid to cry when he is hurt, angry or sorry. He is always transparent, always sincere. And he trusts God.

Not confined by intellectual reasoning, when he comes to Christ, he comes as a child. Kevin seems to know God - to really be friends with Him in a way that is difficult for an 'educated' person to grasp. God seems like his closest companion. In my moments of doubt and frustrations with my Christianity, I envy the security Kevin has in his simple faith. It is then that I am most willing to admit that he has some divine knowledge that rises above my mortal questions.

It is then I realize that perhaps he is not the one with the handicap. I am. My obligations, my fear, my pride, my circumstances - they all become disabilities when I do not trust them to God's care. Who knows if Kevin comprehends things I can never learn? After all, he has spent his whole life in that kind of innocence, praying after dark and soaking up the goodness and love of God. And one day, when the mysteries of heaven are opened, and we are all amazed at how close God really is to our hearts, I'll realize that God heard the simple prayers of a boy who believed that God lived under his bed. Kevin won't be surprised at all!

As I listened to Tony tell me about his brother, tears welled up in my eyes as I remembered one brother in a lodge I belonged to. His name doesn't matter, but he suffered from Lou Gehrig's Disease. I would sit and listen to the same grumbling every time he had to do ritual work on the floor. He would struggle with his words, he had trouble walking in a straight line, and on occasion he would drop his rod on the floor. Older brothers would grumble and complain, still others would comment that we should not advance him in the line of officers and one other individual, who suffered with the same disease, was so indignant that we put him in line, he transferred to another lodge.

But as I watched him work, sweat would roll down his face as he fought to complete the task at hand. His mid was sharp, very sharp and he was very intelligent. It's just that the disease would slow the words down from his brain to his mouth. He worked hard to overcome his physical disability. When he became master, I had the honor to install him and I was so proud. In short, his year was not without its share of problems, but all in all it was very successful.

Watching him and relating it to Kevin's story reminds us that Christ told us we are all branches of the same vine. In other words, we are all part of King Solomon's temple. Some of us have different roles to fulfill but, we all make up the whole.

Each of us is building a Masonic Edifice. All our brothers make up a part of that edifice. They influence us, they teach us, they help us, and some correct us.

Each one adding to the bricks that make the edifice a whole. So, as we look at each one with their uniqueness and different abilities, are we all that different? Aren't we all a part of each other's edifice also? Don't we influence those around us? With this in mind, as you gaze upon the Great Light of Masonry and remember those lessons learned in your obligations, are we all really that different?

CHAPTER 23
Just how We've Always Done It

A group of scientists placed 5 monkeys in a cage and in the middle, a ladder with bananas on top. Every time a monkey went up the ladder, the scientists soaked the rest of the monkeys with cold water. After a while, every time a monkey went up the ladder, the other ones beat up the one on the ladder. After some time, no monkey dare to go up the ladder regardless of the temptation.

Scientists then decided to substitute one of the monkeys. The first thing the new monkey did was go up the ladder. Immediately, the other monkeys beat him up. After several beatings, the new member learned not to climb the ladder even though he never knew why.

The second monkey was substituted, and the same thing occurred. The first monkey participated on the beating for the second monkey. A third monkey was changed and the same was repeated. The fourth was then substituted and the beating was repeated and finally the fifth monkey was replaced. What was left was a group of 5 monkeys that, despite having never received the cold shower, continued to beat up any monkey who attempted to climb the ladder.

If it was possible to ask the monkeys why they would beat up all those who attempted to go up the ladder, the answer would most likely be something to the tune of, "I don't know, that's just how things are around here." Sound familiar?

Do we know someone who might be asking themselves why we continue to do things the same way, even if there's a different, better alternative? I'm sure we do. We all do. In fact, I'd be that you have even asked that same question from time to time. In our lodges do we often get beat up because we wanted to climb the ladder and do things a little different, a little better? Sure. We have all suffered from that. Some more than others. But what we should ask ourselves is whether we beat up the new guy because that wasn't the way we did things and he hasn't been back since. I've seen it not only in our lodges and chapters but in churches also.

So how do we address the situation? How do we get some of the old-time to quit mouthing off or muttering? That answer is as varied as there are people. Each of us is different. Each of us has different things we bring to the party. I am reminded of the teaching found in Hebrews 6:1 (NIV) Therefore let us leave the elementary teachings about Christ and go on to maturity, not laying again the foundation of repentance from acts that lead to death, and of faith in God,

No one can escape coming into the world as a baby because that is the only way to get here! But it is tragic when a baby fails to mature. No matter how much parents and grandparents love to hold and cuddle a baby, it is their great desire that the baby grow up and enjoy a full life as a mature adult. God has the same desire for His children. That is why He calls to us, "Go on to maturity!" (Heb. 6:1, NIV)

It is a call to spiritual progress (vv. 1-3). If we are going to make progress, we have to leave the childhood things behind and go forward in spiritual growth. Hebrews 6:1 literally reads, "Therefore, having left [once and for all] the elementary lessons [the ABCs] of the teaching of Christ." When I was in kindergarten, the teacher taught us our ABCs. (We didn't have television to teach us in those days.) You learn your ABCs so that you might read words, sentences, books—in fact, anything in literature. But you do not keep learning the basics. You use the basics to go on to better things. [Bible Exposition Commentary (BE Series) - New Testament - New Testament, Volume 2.]

Masonry is replete with lessons like this. Some are found directly in the ritual and some are implied through the ritual. Regardless of where we might find the direct lesson, the point is that Masonry requires the mason to mature and read the Volume of Sacred Law. To regard it as the Great Light in Masonry. It is by the application of the lesson found in Hebrews that we can first correct ourselves and our own attitudes before addressing the behavior of our esteemed brethren. Masonry requires that we grow and lead by example. Dou you think that this basic tenant came from the Volume of Sacred Law or was it dreamed up by some overzealous brother?

With this in mind, are you going to keep beating up the new monkeys or are you going to help him climb the ladder and ward off the others who would beat him up?

CHAPTER 24

THE LAMBSKIN APRON

This article has, as its backdrop and adoption, the Masonic Service Associations SHORT TALK BULLETIN - Vol. V November 1927 No.11: The original author of this work is Unknown.

In Masonic symbolism the Lambskin Apron holds priority. It is the first of the initial gifts of Freemasonry to a candidate, and at the end of life's pilgrimage it is reverently placed on his mortal remains to be buried with his body in the grave.

Above all other symbols, the Lambskin Apron is the most distinguishing emblem of Masonry. Some Masonic writers contend that the initiation ceremony is representative of birth into moral truth and spiritual faith. Much has been written in ancient teachings which has shown an effort that the Lambskin Apron also typifies regeneration or a new life. The basis of which might have been the story of Laban and Jacob as found in Genesis 29 and 30 where he separated out the flocks for division between them thus giving Jacob a new start with his wives and children.

This thought and incorporating the ideas along the lines of resurrection might be the cause of its intended burial with the body of a deceased brother. The association of the lamb with redemption and being born again is expressed by John, the Apocalyptic Seer, who had a vision on the Isle of Patmos, and beheld the purified and redeemed "Of All Nations, Kindreds, People and Tongues." Of them it was said, "These are they which came out of great tribulation and have washed their robes and made them white in the blood of the Lamb." As found in Revelation 7:9.

Over the years, masons have been regarded as one of the religious symbols we use today. In our present theology there are three parts of man; body, soul and spirit; what the body is to the soul, the soul to the spirit; namely, a house or habitation, but, in many far-eastern religions they have developed a thought that there are seven parts of man; four earthly and three heavenly; four physical and three spiritual. Applying that theology to the apron we could deduce that the four sides of the square symbolize the four physical and the three sides of the flap, or triangle, symbolize the three spiritual parts of man. The apex of the triangle, or point of the flap, could stand for the Atma, and which means the eternal spark, the Divine Flame, the indestructible spirit of the living God in every human being but, most Christian Masons use it as a representation of the Holy Trinity or Tri-Unity of God the Father, God the Son and God the Holy Spirit. With this in mind, we can assert that it means God is not a looker on the Life of anyone; and God is is a part of every man.

A badge is either good or bad by reason of that for which it stands. Aside from mysticism, I believe there are five distinct things of which the Lambskin Apron is a badge.

Firstly, in its use, it is a badge of service. In his recent book on "Symbolical Masonry," Brother H.L. Haywood has an interesting chapter on "The Apron wherein the Builder Builds," and says it "was so conspicuous a portion of the costume of an operative Mason that it became associated with him in the public mind and thus gradually evolved into his badge." By it Speculative Freemasonry seeks to distinguish the builder and place upon the brow of labor the laurel wreath of dignity and honor.

Secondly, made of lambskin, it is in its fabric a badge of sacrifice. The lamb in all ages has been not only an emblem of innocence, but also a symbol of sacrifice, and he who wears this Apron with understanding must be prepared for the time when hard things are to be done, when trials are to be endured, and fortitude glorified. Thirdly, in its color it is a badge of purity. White is the clean color that reflects most light.

In Masonry there are three great religious rites. One is discalceation, that is, entering a holy place or standing in the presence of God barefooted as a symbol of humility. It comes from a time where the memory of man does not run to the contrary. When God appeared to Moses in the burning bush, he said, "Put off thy shoes from thy feet for the place where you stand is holy ground." Another is the rite of circumambulation, that it, going around an Altar from east to west by way of the south. Dr. Joseph Fort Newton said: "When man emerged from the night of barbarism his religion was a worship of light; to him light was life and love, darkness was evil and death; to him light was the mother of beauty, the unveiler of color, the radiant, illusive mystery of the world; his Temple was hung with stars, his Altar a glowing flame, his ritual a woven hymn of night and day." To him the sun was the greatest of God's creations, it inspired his adoration and in all his religious ceremonies he followed its apparent course through the heavens, as though he were walking in the footsteps of the Most High. Through this rite, memories of that religion of the dawn linger with us in Masonry today.

The third is the rite of investiture or purification; that is, the presentation of the Apron. In a qualified way it bears the relationship to the Lodge that baptism does to some Churches, it is the external symbol of an inner purification. The Psalmist asked:

"Who shall ascend into the Hill of the Lord?" and answering his own question said, "He that hath clean hands and a pure heart." The Apron when correctly understood is the pledge of a clean life, the testimony that a candidate means to live pure, speak true, and right with his reverence conscience as a guide.

When we turn to the Ritual for its interpretation, we find the Apron to be an inheritance from the past, it is a badge of antiquity, "more ancient than the Golden Fleece and Roman Eagle." A ministerial Brother once said, "That the Masonic Ritual was couched in stilted phrases and extravagant language, and, as an illustration referred to the ritualistic speech used in the presentation of the Apron." Let us see if he was right. The most specific way of conveying thought and expressing truth is by comparison, it is difficult to comprehend an idea unless we can correlate or compare it with something already known. The Order of the Golden Fleece referred to was founded in the year 1429, by Phillip, Duke of Burgundy; the Roman Eagle became Rome's Ensign of Imperial Power about one century before the Christian era, while the Apron had come down to us from the very sunrise of time. "Hebrew Prophets often wore Aprons," they were called a "A Prophets Mantle" and were also used in the ancient mysteries of India and Egypt. They were used by early Chinese secret societies, by the Jewish religious sect called Essenes, they were employed as emblems by the Incas of Peru, the Aztecs of Mexico, and the prehistoric races of the American continent.

As a badge of antiquity, it emphasizes the value of the past. Blackstone, in his commentaries on the English Law, said, "That in the making of a new law three things must be considered: namely, the old law, the mischief and the remedy. No man can apply an intelligent remedy to an existing mischief without regard to the antecedent conditions out of which it grew." He continues, "Present progress must be based on the accumulated experience and wisdom of the ages." Albert Pike said, "It is the dead who govern, the living only obey." "Every ship that comes to America got its chart from Columbus, every novel is debtor to Homer, every carpenter who shaves with a foreplane borrows the genius of some forgotten inventor."

As a badge of antiquity, the Apron exalts the greatness and glory of the past in its present contribution to human good and happiness. In the fifth place, the Apron is a badge of honor. It is declared to be "More honorable than the Star and Garter." Here there is another comparison. The Order of the Star and Garter was created by John II of France at the beginning of his reign in the middle of the 14th century. It was a Royal plaything and at the time of its formation its founder was engaged in acts of despotism and destruction.

The Order of the Garter was formed by Edward III of England in 1349. It was composed of the King and Twenty-five knights and originated in the egotism and fantastic pomp and circumstance of medieval manners. Edward A. Freeman, an English historian says: "The spirit of knighthood is above all things a class spirit. The good knight is bound to endless courtesies toward men and women of a certain rank; and he may treat all below that rank with any degree of scorn and cruelty." "Chivalry is in morals what feudalism is in law.

Each substitutes personal obligations devised in the interest of an exclusive class, for the more homey duties of an honest man and a good citizen."

Freemasonry is in striking contrast to such conceptions. It stands for the uprightness of discord and dissension, for the promotion of peace, the pursuit of knowledge and the practice of brotherhood, for untrammeled conscience, equality of opportunity and the Divine right of liberty in man, for devotion to duty, the building of character and rectitude of life and conduct. It has as its symbolical supports; wisdom, strength and beauty; the principal basis of its theological ladder is faith, hope and charity. Its primary tenets are brotherly love, relief and truth and its cardinal virtues are fortitude, prudence and justice. Its Temple is erected to the Master Builder; its Great Light is the Word of Revelation. Resting on the representation of the Altar of high and Holy purpose. The spirit of Freemasonry is like the shadow of a rock in a weary land, like a shining light in a window of a home, like a mother's kiss on a trouble brow and the breath of her prayer in the hour of despair, calling men from the circumference of life to find God at the center of the Mason's individual soul.

"When we consider the messages delivered by these Orders and the Lambskin Apron - one speaking the language of class distinction, special privilege and the Divine right of Kings; the other telling the story of exact justice, equality of opportunity, and the brotherhood of man - it is not a stilted phrase and an exaggeration of speech, to say that the badge of a Mason is more honorable than the Star and Garter." As a badge of honor, the Lambskin Apron spells out integrity, honesty of purpose, probity of character, and soundness of moral principle.

CHAPTER 25
ARE THERE MISSING STONES IN MASONRY?

The rituals used in modern speculative freemasonry included some comprehensive lectures on the working tools used by operative freemasons, but the writers have omitted some other important elements of the ancient symbolism, especially in respect to the stones used in the buildings. In most of the degrees of operative freemasonry, that being the different levels of obtaining being a master craftsman, the candidate, always represents a particular stone, either during the course of its preparation or while it was being fixed into position. In this context the plans and gauges used during the preparation and erection of the stones also were of symbolic importance. It also helped the operative mason to understand the lesson being taught but the morality that was expected by his guild. The rough and perfect ashlars and the keystone are important symbols in the speculative craft and the mark degrees found in the York Rite.

The reasons why the rough ashlar represents an apprentice and the perfect ashlar represents the more expert craftsman become self-evident as we explore the lessons taught and the expectations that were part of his position. It also is common knowledge among operative masons that a specially shaped keystone is useful as well as being a pleasing embellishment with which to complete the construction of an arch. This stone had, in some cases crests of the owner, or other emblems engraved on the faces. Some were a slightly larger stone in dimensions to stand out from the structure of the arch since they were placed at the apex of the arch. However, many speculative freemasons are not aware of these or several other important stones and their symbolic meanings much less their actual usage in the construction of an edifice. Nor do they receive any explanation of the meanings of the various plan shapes used in buildings. Some of these aspects will be looked at briefly, in order to help the inquisitive mason achieve a better understanding of important lessons conveyed by the speculative rituals.

It is probably worth noting that a cubical stone is rarely used in masonry structures except to complete a course adjacent to openings. We sometimes hear them referred to as a half-stone today. Nevertheless, it was an important stone used to test the skills of an apprentice who wanted to become a fully qualified fellowcraft of the trade, when his knowledge of the various projections of a cube was also tested. In ancient times another use of a cubical stone was as the great corner stone, sometimes used to stabilize the corner of a building and placed in the North-east corner as a reference to square This stone is referred to in Isaiah 28:16, (NIV)

"So this is what the Sovereign LORD says: See, I lay a stone in Zion, a tested stone, a precious cornerstone for a sure foundation; the one who trusts will never be dismayed." Which is an allusion or prophecy of the coming messiah. It is also quoted in I Peter 2:6-8 (NIV)

"For in Scripture it says: See, I lay a stone in Zion, a chosen and precious cornerstone, and the one who trusts in him will never be put to shame. Now to you who believe, this stone is precious. But to those who do not believe, the stone the builders rejected has become the capstone, and, a stone that causes men to stumble and a rock that makes them fall. They stumble because they disobey the message-- which is also what they were destined for." This is also a reference to Christ.

The more stable and commonly used method of securing the corners of a large masonry structure is with what is called an elbow square stone. These are right angled stones which have one leg four units long and the other leg three units long, each leg being square in cross-section with sides of one unit. Don Falconer noted English Freemason and scholar says, "It therefore is like a Pythagorean triangle without an hypotenuse." He continues, "We find that they are placed with the long and short legs alternating in successive courses at the corners, with the wall stones securely fixed in between them." The operative mason passes the lesson on that these stones should be a reminder that our work must be properly squared in compliance with the plans laid down in the scriptures or The Great Light of Masonry.

You math heads will like the fact that most of the stones used in the construction of masonry walls are called running stones. These are usually square in cross-section with a length three times the sectional dimension. Although a length of twice the sectional dimension may be used. The stones are staggered, as in brickwork, in alternate courses to avoid concurrent joints being formed in successive courses. This small detail could be detrimental to the strength of the structure if these were in a straight line. These stones remind us that we are in need to work in harmony with our fellow man and that in all we do, it must be straight, level and true. The footing corner stone is another especially important stone in masonry structures. It is a tee-shaped stone has the top of the tee in equal length to two running stones and the other leg the same length as the section dimension. This sectional dimension naturally must be the same as that of the running stones which will be joined to it. The usual placement of this stone is in alternate courses where an external wall meets at the junction with an internal wall. This is done so that the running stones in both walls mesh with the projecting legs of the tee. This stone reminds us that our strength is a united effort, while its shape, which is just happens to be that of a Tau cross, emphasizes the importance of serving the Lord. We read in Ezekiel 9:4 we are told that this was the mark to be placed on the foreheads of those to be saved. Ezekiel 9:4 (NIV)

"and said to him, "Go throughout the city of Jerusalem and put a mark on the foreheads of those who grieve and lament over all the detestable things that are done in it."

Ezekiel 9:4

Set a mark upon the foreheads of the men that sigh—This is in allusion to the ancient every-where-used custom of setting marks on servants and slaves, to distinguish them from others. It was also common for the worshippers of particular idols to have their idol's mark upon their foreheads, arms, etc. These are called sectarian marks to the present day among the Hindus and others in India. Hence by this mark we can easily know who is a follower of Vishnoo, who of Siva, who of Bramah, etc. The original words, והתוית תו vehithvitha tau, have been translated by the Vulgate, et signa thau, "and mark thou tau on the foreheads," etc. St. Jerome and many others have thought that the letter tau was the symbol that was ordered to be placed on the foreheads of those mourners; and Jerome says, that this Hebrew letter ת tau was formerly written like a cross. So then the people were to be signed with the sign of the cross! It is certain that on the ancient Samaritan coins, which are yet extant, the letter ת tau is in the form +, which is what we term St. Andrew's cross. The sense derived from this by many commentators is, that God, having ordered those penitents to be marked with this figure, which is the sign of the cross, intimated that there is no redemption nor saving of life but by the cross of Christ, and that this will avail none but the real penitent. All this is true in itself, but it is not true in respect to this place. The Hebrew words signify literally, thou shalt make a mark, or sign a sign, but give no intimation what that mark or sign was. It was intended here to be what the sprinkling of the blood of the paschal lamb on the lintels and doorposts of the Israelites was, namely, a notice to the destroying angel what house he should spare. This symbolical action teaches us that God, in general judgments, will make a distinction between the innocent and the guilty, between the penitent and the hardened sinner.

This is why we, we as Masons, are taught to Square our actions. We are the building blocks of our fraternity and as such we need to display the qualities that living stones should have by using real building stones as representations.

CHAPTER 26
Matthew 7:7 Ask, Seek, and Knock

"In all human affairs there are efforts, and there are results, and the strength of the effort is the measure of the result." [9]

In your initiation into Freemasonry, you received a lecture in the first degree which quoted Matthew 7:7. Not too many masons will remember that unless you happened to be one of the few that have memorized the lecture it was quoted in. And I'm sure that most have not even thought about what the actual meaning is. This is one of the interesting things about Masonic Ritual. It contains a bunch of nuggets like this to light our path.

Anyway, the verse reads: Matthew 7:7 (KJV) "Ask, and it shall be given you; seek, and ye shall find; knock, and it shall be opened unto you." There is an old story about how the University of Chicago received a million-dollar grant from the heiress of a major department store. She had been a student at Northwest. So, administrators of Northwest went to visit her and asked why she had not made such a gift to her alma mater. Her answer was simple, "The people at the University of Chicago asked. You did not."

Looking at this lesson from the Biblical perspective, as Jesus approached the end of his discourse on the Galilean hillside, he gives yet another surprising and puzzling teaching:

---

[9] James Allen. Favorite. James Allen (2013). "As a Man Thinketh & The Way of Peace", p.20, Simon and Schuster

Matthew 7:7-11 ESV "Ask, and it will be given to you; seek, and you will find; knock, and it will be opened to you. For everyone who asks receives, and the one who seeks finds, and to the one who knocks it will be opened. Or which one of you, if his son asks him for bread, will give him a stone? Or if he asks for a fish, will give him a serpent? If you then, who are evil, know how to give good gifts to your children, how much more will your Father who is in heaven give good things to those who ask him! Here Jesus introduces a new aspect of interaction with God.

Speaking to his disciples as they passed by the fruitless fig tree – now withered – this happened: Mark 11:21-24 ESV And Peter remembered and said to him, "Rabbi, look! The fig tree that you cursed has withered." And Jesus answered them, "Have faith in God. (Note: the original Kione Greek Literal Translations says, "Have God's Faith."). Truly, I say to you, whoever says to this mountain, 'Be taken up and thrown into the sea,' and does not doubt in his heart, but believes that what he says will come to pass, it will be done for him. Therefore, I tell you, whatever you ask in prayer, believe that you have received it, and it will be yours. He seems to say there's nothing God won't do if you merely ask. Is that really Jesus' meaning?

It reminds me of a story in the wild west about the cowboy that rode into a town seriously threatened by drought. The town came together and decided to have a chain prayer, and when the cowboy's turn came to say the words, he decided that instead of praying for rain, he would take a short cut and pray for all the things they needed. "Lord, give us barrels of flour, ... barrels of potatoes, ... barrels of corn, ... barrels of tomatoes, ... barrels of cabbage, ... barrels of onions, ... barrels of salt, ... barrels of pepper."

One of the men of the town nudged the cowboy and said, "Way too much pepper, Cowboy." Has your Masonic experience always been that every time you ask something of the lodge, a brother, or of God, you get exactly what you asked for, you find the very thing you seek, and that every closed door is opened if you knock?

The experience of every person reveals that we are not granted every request. We need to understand whether Jesus promises that, in every situation, our requests will be blindly granted – no qualifiers, conditions, or limitations - or if instead, he is laying down a broad principle. Or that it is true within a certain frame of reference but untrue outside of it. For if we do not understand what Jesus means, we are likely to have false expectations certain to fail, and we will wonder what is wrong – and perhaps blame ourselves for not believing firmly enough that our request will be granted or worse yet blame others.

Is a lack of intensity in belief on our part always the reason when our requests are denied – or might something else be the reason? Do we see that with the thing we are trying to get accomplished in lodge? What is going on when we ask, seek, and knock, and whatever we seek is not forthcoming? James gives one answer: James 4:1-3 ESV "What causes quarrels and what causes fights among you? Is it not this, that your passions are at war within you? You desire and do not have, so you murder. You covet and cannot obtain, so you fight and quarrel. You do not have, because you do not ask. You ask and do not receive, because you ask wrongly, to spend it on your passions." Do we see that in lodge?

This scripture is applicable within the intended frame of reference. A thing can be true within the intended frame of reference, but false outside that framework. While the reason James gave his readers was true about the persons James wrote this letter to, I suggest that James' answer is not universally applicable. On a worldwide scale across the centuries, more is more involved than James intended to answer in this letter. Specifically, he wrote to the 12 tribes in the dispersion - people James knew a lot about. The fact that some of them were driven by their lusts and passions to make selfish requests does not necessarily mean that you have been driven by your lusts when you pray for a gravely ill sick one to recover – and they die anyway. But if your prayers are driven by your own lusts and passions, the teaching is applicable to you.

Isaiah wrote God's own words about God's very thoughts: Isaiah 55:7-9 ESV "let the wicked forsake his way, and the unrighteous man his thoughts; let him return to the Lord, that he may have compassion on him, and to our God, for he will abundantly pardon. For my thoughts are not your thoughts, neither are your ways my ways, declares the Lord. For as the heavens are higher than the earth, so are my ways higher than your ways and my thoughts than your thoughts."

Sometimes a parent denies a child's request. God knows better than we what we need, what we desire, and what is fit for us. We should never suppose that God would bid us to pray, and then give us what would be hurtful. Do we see someone act out something similar in lodge? They don't get their way so they take it out on everyone else? God is not an automaton, recklessly obeying our requests, no matter how misguided and selfish. Nor is Jesus, by giving this assurance on the mountain, making God our servant! Often times in Masonry we want to make some of our brethren our servants instead of being a servant to them. Then does Jesus' statement, "Ask and you shall receive..." suggest that when we ask God for something it is set aside - not because we ask for the purpose of feeding our lusts - but because it conflicts with a higher purpose, or overrides the protective care of a Father for a child? It seems so. The desires of men do not supersede the wisdom and the plans of God. I see us supplanting the leadership of lodges and Grand Lodges with this same type of attitude. They want to supplant and supersede the plans which have been laid by the master and by God. Let's consider where the scriptures tell us exactly that.

Jesus prayed, "If it is possible, let this cup pass from me, yet not as I will, but your will be done." (Matthew 26:39)

2 Cor 12:1f - Paul (v8) three times requested that it be removed. Instead, the Lord told him, "My grace is sufficient for you, for my power is made perfect in weakness." God will always answer our prayers. In one form or another. We may not like the answer, but He answers in the way a wise, loving parent responds to the requests of a child--sometimes by supplying something better than was requested, and sometimes by denying it altogether. Then does praying make any difference, or does God give us what we ask only if it is what he was going to do anyway, even if we didn't ask? Do we have any influence with God?

James 5:16 Confess your trespasses to one another, and pray for one another, that you may be healed. The effective, fervent prayer of a righteous man avails much. I think in lodges we miss the boat here.

We fail to unite and confide in each other for the common good of the lodge. Over the years, we have slowly taken praying out of the lodge. I remember the master, when I was going through the line the first time ask the chaplain for prayer on multiple occasions for our goals, money making projects, and etc.

Yes, we have influence with God, but these passages do not suggest that our wants and wishes obligate God to fulfill every request as a demand as if we are the master and he the servant. Continuing with probably the most familiar part of the sermon, Jesus says:

Matthew 7:12 ESV "So whatever you wish that others would do to you, do also to them, for this is the Law and the Prophets." The word "So" in ESV ("therefore" on other translations) is actually in the text, from a word that means, "accordingly," or "likewise then." The conjunction "so" shows that this statement is related to what Jesus had most recently said. It is the conclusion to which Jesus' prior teaching in the sermon on the mount leads. Jesus' teaching - commonly called "the golden rule" refers to Lev 19:18 -ESV "You shall not take vengeance or bear a grudge against the sons of your own people, but you shall love your neighbor as yourself: I am the LORD."

The second great commandment is the same ethic as what Jesus said on the mountain. There is no daylight between loving our neighbor as ourselves and – as Jesus says - doing to others as we wish them to do unto us. Loving is the force that drives the doing. So let me ask you this, "Are we, as lodge and as individuals, asking for our neighbors, brethren and the lodge, or are we being selfish in our prayers assuming God will answer them the way we want?"

An illustration of how not to act toward our neighbor is given by James (2:2-10), where he speaks of treating a man who comes into the meeting in shabby clothes. If we treat such a one with less dignity than a rich man who comes into the assembly, we are not applying "the royal law," which says, Love your neighbor as yourself. We do this in lodge all the time. I see this in the churches, in other Masonic bodies. It appears we have taken Matthew 7:7 from the ritual and the Great Light of Masonry totally out of context and applied it ourselves only.

This rule of life is more than an ethic which says, "What is harmful to another, I will not do." "Do no harm" is a cardinal rule of practice for physicians (and nurses and others in the medical profession?). "Do no harm" is benign, but it is only the negative side of this rule. It's important, but it's not the only decision a physician has to make. A physician whose only rule is "do no harm" would not help a patient for fear of violating that ethic. To practice the rule positively, you must not only be harmless, but beneficial to others. Setting aside self-interest, actively do for others what we would have them do for us. By doing this simple but seemingly complicated little thing, it brings the true meaning of Ask, Seek, and Knock into perspective. The application of which now would be more in line of what masonry teaches us.

CHAPTER 27
JACOBS LADDER

The Masonic ritual is replete with numerous examples and signposts for further enlightenment. One of those signposts is found in the first-degree lecture. The paragraph is describing the covering of the lodge is no less that the clouded canopy or star decked heaven, where all good Freemasons hope at last to arrive by aid of that theological ladder which Jacob, in his vision, saw extending from earth to heaven… Let's take a look this lesson from the Great light of Masonry. We find the story of Jacob's Ladder in Genesis 28:12, however, it actually begins in Genesis 26 and he really starts to muddy things up in chapter 27.

So, Isaac sent Jacob away, and he went to Padan Aram, to Laban the son of Bethuel the Syrian, the brother of Rebekah, the mother of Jacob and Esau. Esau saw that Isaac had blessed Jacob and sent him away to Padan Aram to take himself a wife from there, and that as he blessed him he gave him a charge, saying, "You shall not take a wife from the daughters of Canaan," and that Jacob had obeyed his father and his mother and had gone to Padan Aram. Because Rebekah knew that Esau was intending to kill him. But before Isaac sent Jacob away, he confirmed the blessing on him, and then sent him off to Haran, so that he could find a wife from Rebekah's family. But now, Jacob is on his own. And I don't know about y'all, but I see Jacob as one of those guys who doesn't like to be alone. He's one of those guys who needs attention from others. Are we sometimes like that when it comes to lodge functions? Do we need the company of our brothers to fill in some gaps that may be missing in our lives?

But here he is all by himself now. He's isolated. And it's dark. So, Jacob decides to set up a makeshift camp, and rest through the night. He took one of the stones of that place and put it at his head, and he lay down in that place to sleep. The place he has come to is Bethel.

The name literally means, "the House of God." Bethel is twelve miles north of Jerusalem and the home which Jacob left was probably twenty-five or thirty miles south of Jerusalem.

This means that Jacob covered at least forty miles that first day. You can see that he was really hotfooting it away from Esau. He wants to get as far from him as he can, but the farther he gets away from Esau, the farther he gets away from home.

Bethel is a dreary place. It has been described as highlands with large, bare rocks exposed. It's twelve hundred feet above sea level, in the hills. Next, we are told that Jacob fell asleep…and all of a sudden, he has a dream.

Then he dreamed, and behold, a ladder was set up on the earth, and its top reached to heaven; and there the angels of God were ascending and descending on it. And behold, the Lord stood above it and said: "I am the Lord God of Abraham your father and the God of Isaac; the land on which you lie I will give to you and your descendants. Also your descendants shall be as the dust of the earth; you shall spread abroad to the west and the east, to the north and the south; and in you and in your seed all the families of the earth shall be blessed."

Now God is giving to Jacob exactly what He had given first to Abraham; He had repeated it to Isaac, and now he confirms it, and He reaffirms to Jacob that He will do this. Then God said, "Behold, I am with you and will keep you wherever you go, and will bring you back to this land; for I will not leave you until I have done what I have spoken to you." You can see that this would be comforting and helpful to a lonesome, homesick boy who really had to leave home in a hurry. I am sure many of us find that kind of comfort from the brothers we grow closer to in lodge. We develop friendships which can fill a much-needed void in our lives. We Jacob is on his way to a far country, and this first night God says to him, "I'm going to be with you, Jacob, and I'm going to bring you back to this land." The vision that God gave to him in the dream was of a ladder that reached up to heaven. What does the ladder mean? To the Christian, regardless of denomination, the ladder is Christ. The angels are ascending and descending upon the Son of Man. The angels ministered to Him; they were subject to His command. The Lord Jesus said, "…I am the way, the truth, and the life: no man comes unto the Father, but by me."

The Lord Jesus Christ Himself is the ladder—not one that we can climb, but one that we can trust. However, it could be speculated that Jacob viewed the ladder in this way. I believe he saw it as a way or a tool of communication from God to him. Then Jacob awoke from his sleep and said, "Surely the Lord is in this place, and I did not know it." And he was afraid and said, "How awesome is this place! This is none other than the house of God, and this is the gate of heaven!"

After God appears to him in this dream, Jacob wakes up and he responds by worshiping. He builds an altar and worships the Lord. And he calls the place "Bethel" which literally means "The House of God!" So, he's doing pretty good up until that point, but then he makes a vow, and you notice; it's a conditional vow. A point to consider: Did you make a conditional vow or obligation? Did your obligation have any of the "if you do this; I'll do that" promises buried inside? Mine did not. It was an obligation to others. An obligation to myself with no bartering. Notice what Jacob does next.

He says, "God if you'll be with me, and watch over me, and feed me and provide clothing for me, and make sure that I come back home in peace, THEN the LORD will be my God, and not only that, I'll be come a faithful tither." Basically he's saying, "God if You do what You just told me You'll do, then You'll be my God." And there's a couple of things here I want you to see.

First of all, God is just. And being that He's just, He is going to judge, based on truth and knowledge. We find in the New Testament, Zacharias is told that he is going to have a son and that he is to name him John (Luke 1), Zacharias has doubts and is made unable to talk for the next 9 months. But here, Jacob is expressing doubt, and putting conditions on God, and nothing happens to him. But the thing to remember is, Zacharias was a priest. He had been taught the Scriptures from the time he was a little boy. Note that at time the Scriptures consisted of what we call the Pentateuch or the first five books of our current Bible. Zacharias knew about God, and He knew that God keeps His Word. He was a believer and a teacher... Jacob on the other hand, was a little different. We can tell from the Scriptures that his knowledge of God was limited at best.

He wasn't a priest of any kind. He wasn't a teacher of God's Word. In-fact, they didn't even have any Scriptures at this time... They wouldn't until Moses wrote them down by inspiration of the Holy Spirit. So, Jacob didn't have the luxury of opening his Bible and double checking what he had experienced in this dream. And this is important to us because we do have God's Word. The Great Light of Masonry. And we live in a nation that is greatly influenced by the Bible, and Biblical principles and morality.

So right here, Jacob is given a pass, because of his ignorance... later on, more is required of him. But all of us sitting here today, we can't claim ignorance. In-fact; if anyone in the United States of America is ignorant about God, it's due to willful ignorance, and willful ignorance is no excuse.

The second thing is Jacob's mention of the tithe. The giving of a tenth. Now contrary to what some people might think here, Jacob's not being a cheap skate. He's not saying, "God if you do all this for me, I can manage giving you 1/10th of everything I have." Because if you look at verse 22 again, you'll notice that he says, "God, all that YOU GIVE me, I will return a tenth to you." In other words, Jacob was saying, "God if it is You who are giving me these things, and if it's You who are blessing me. Then it's no big deal for me to give back to You a tenth."

Jacob might have been a lot of things, but he understood worship, and he understood ownership. He understood that if God gave it, then God could take it away, and he understood that if it was God who was giving it, then that was the only reason he would have it in the first place. So, what you and I have, and what we have been blessed with, is from the Lord. If we have any success in life; we should never, ever think that we are the ones who are responsible for it. God gave us our minds, our ability to work, our health, and everything we have, and we should be thankful and grateful.

We have seen only one viewpoint and one possible explanation of Jacob's Ladder found in our ritual. The paragraph also says it has three principle rounds Faith, Hope and Charity. We have covered Faith and Hope somewhat in this discussion. Charity is always a lengthy discussion and has many examples as do the other two. I hope that by this brief look and Jacob's Ladder it gives a better idea of some of the nuggets of wisdom and rays of light contained within the Masonic ritual. For further reading or if you want to do your own study of the ladder read the story of Jacob in Genesis. His story is not only interesting but is also peppered with nuggets of wisdom from the Grand Architect of the Universe.

CHAPTER 28

A CERTAIN POINT

"… there is represented in every regular and well-governed Lodge a certain point within a circle embordered by two perpendicular parallel lines, … and upon the vertex of the circle rests the Holy Bible." Introduced to mason in the Entered Apprentice degree lecture, it is expanded in the 12th degree of the Scottish Rite -- if we look closely enough at what is being taught, the lesson taught in the EA degree is the beginning of "circumscribing our desires and keeping our passions within due bounds" as expanded upon in the MM degree. However, it is noted that the point within the circle represents an individual brother and that at the vertex rests the Holy Bible. In other degrees we are taught that the point could represent the North Star or fixed compass heading. It could also represent our Deity in whom we should make the center of our universe and His word rests upon the vertex of the circle.

Examining the concept that the point represents an individual, we can quickly see that he is surrounded by area encompassing him which is contained within the boundaries of the circle. This could beg the question as to what is the area and what does it represent? A look at Christianity could conclude that the area the individual is contained in could be the Spirit of God, otherwise referred to as the Holy Spirit. With this in mind, it could be concluded that the individual mason is not only influenced by the Word of God found at the apex of the circle but by God's direction through the Holy Spirit. This picture would allow us to see how the influence of the

Holy Spirit would keep our passions within due bounds as we progress through life.

A look at Judaism would or could afford us the same view. It could be argued on behalf of the Hebrews that the boundaries that were established by the confines of the circle are the teaching and prophetic announcements brought forth by the prophets of Israel. These prophets not only gave the prophecies that God gave them to tell the people but also their meaning in most cases. In each case when the meaning was given it applied to the individual receiving the prophecy and the nation, but to all the people as its effects would be noticed and felt throughout the kingdom. We see some of this concerning Solomon and the prophet Nathan, Elijah and the Elisha, Joseph and Nebuchadnezzar, and so forth. We could also apply this to the teaching of Christ in the Christian.

The teachings of Jesus not only affect each one of us individually but as a collective the entire world. We learn in Scripture from 2 Timothy 3:16-17 (KJV) that "All scripture is given by inspiration of God, and is profitable for doctrine, for reproof, for correction, for instruction in righteousness: That the man of God may be perfect, thoroughly furnished unto all good works." Isn't this verse of the Great Light of Masonry applicable to the point within the circle. This verse shows the heart of the meaning of what the symbol can represent.

We as masons are taught early on that the Great Light of Masonry is our rule and guide of our faith, so therefore, as such, it becomes clear that this verse is the central theme of the symbol. It becomes clear that the meaning is contained within the lecture that is given to us when we are receiving the degree. We are pointed to the symbol and told what it stands for. It is up to us to explore its implications as it applies to our lives. The further we grow in masonry, the more light we obtain and the application of that certain point within the circle becomes multi-faceted.

As we have seen thus far, keeping God or our deity as the center point of our lives is key. On the other hand, one could argue that keeping the Word of God at the apex is like the North Star the mariners used in determining their position. A look at the not-too-distant past reveals to us that our founding mariners used the North Star as the fixed point in the heavens to make their navigational headings and their position on the seas. These mariners knew where the North Star was all the time and used it as the guide and main compass heading for due north. It is by this example that we as masons should use the center point of the circle as a North Star so to speak. In Judaism and Christianity, we find the North Star represents God. In other religions it would represent their deity.

"Wisdom is the true light of Masonry." This simple phrase has such a profound truth in its content. We have been looking at the point within a circle and the fact that the point could represent man, God, or the North Star and what the North Star represents to us. I pose this for your consideration. "Wisdom is the true light of Masonry" is the motto of the 12th degree in the Scottish Rite but we are introduced to that concept in the third degree of the Blue Lodge and as such if we incorporate this into our discussion then we can arrive at another conclusion.

If the point represents a brother and the vertex represents the True Heading, we find the source of all wisdom resting upon the vertex of the circle. Both Jew and Christian are reminded that the Holy Word of God rests upon the vertex of the circle and that our true compass heading in life will be contained between the parallel lines and that the Holy Word becomes our constant sextant for finding our current position and defining the direction our lives by maintaining our course between the parallel lines and constantly seeking His Holy Word for our directional headings. We masons are taught throughout all our degrees to seek out God's Word for wisdom and knowledge. The word then becomes our True North and the compasses by which we guide our lives. It helps us to keep our passions in due bounds with all mankind especially a brother master mason.

CHAPTER 29
LIVING STONES

Joe Minor stood erect, in the Northeast corner of the room carefully listening to words of the Master of the lodge whom he had just met minutes before hand. Standing before Joe in his pressed suit and black hat, he appeared to be a good two feet taller than he actually was. Soft and yet commanding his voice impressed the most inactive of emotions and yet Joe's mind raced and he heard the words:

"...But we as Free and Accepted Masons make use of it for the more noble and glorious purpose of divesting our hearts and consciousnesses of all the vices and superfluities of life; thereby fitting our minds as living stones, for that spiritual building, that house not made with hands; eternal in the heavens." (1st degree working tools, Common Gavel.)

Joe, a devout Christian, had heard pros and cons about Masonry. Since his father was a Mason along with his grandfather, he decided to keep the family tradition and join also. He could not concentrate on what instructions and lessons he heard from then on. Those words kept ringing in his ears like the tune of a familiar song. They were from the Bible he thought but where? As he scanned his Instruction Book from the Lord, he came across 1 Peter 2:4 - 8 (NIV)" As you come to him, the living Stone—rejected by men but chosen by God and precious to him— you also, like living stones, are being built into a spiritual house to be a holy priesthood, offering spiritual sacrifices acceptable to God through Jesus Christ. For in Scripture it says: "See,

I lay a stone in Zion, a chosen and precious cornerstone, and the one who trusts in him will never be put to shame." Now to you who believe, this stone is precious. But to those who do not believe, "The stone the builders rejected has become the capstone, "and, "A stone that causes men to stumble and a rock that makes them fall." They stumble because they disobey the message—which is also what they were destined for."

So, what did he actually mean? Joe learned that every building has a cornerstone which, since time in memorial has been laid in the Northeast corner of the edifice as the foundation stone upon which the rest of the building is erected. That stone has to be perfectly square and smooth, without blemish. If the corner stone has a blemish or is out of square that trait is carried throughout the building and will magnify the error.

We learn from verse 2:4 "Him, a living stone." I.e., Christ; cf. 1 Cor 10:4. The spiritual Rock from whom the Apostles drank. And Chosen and precious.

In Verse 2:5 Living stones ... yourselves. As revealed in Mt 16:18. A Spiritual house. In which he told Peter that He would build his Church upon that foundation and the Gates of Hell would not overcome it. The image of the church as God's building, or temple, is common in the New Testament; see 1 Cor 3:16; Eph 2:19-22; 1 Tim 3:15; Heb 12:18-24; Rev 3:12; 11:1. A holy priesthood. The metaphor shifts from believers as living stones composing God's building to believers as those who serve within God's building; cf. Ex 19:6; Rev 1:6; 5:10; also Rom 15:16; Heb 13:10.

We also learn from 2:6 that the quotation is from Isa 28:16, with the same variation as in Rom 9:33. States that God has chosen a Corner Stone, a sure foundation.

Verse 2:7 shifts from the Corner Stone to the Cap Stone and the quotation is from Ps 118:22; cf. Mk 12:10-11; Mt 21:42; Lk 20:17; Acts 4:11. This basically describes the Archway that was common in doorways and halls. The Cap Stone is also called a Key Stone and all of the pressure from the columns and pilasters are directed to that particular stone and locks the edifice solid. This stone, if removed, would cause a collapse of that part of the building.

2:8 The quotation is from Isa 8:14-15 (14 and he will be a sanctuary; but for both (Current conjecture defines this as Jews and Muslims in which both descended from Abraham. Some believe that it means the House of David from the Tribe of Judah and the Levites which were the priestly order for the Jews) houses of Israel he will be a stone that causes men to stumble and a rock that makes them fall. And for the people of Jerusalem he will be a trap and a snare.)

As they were destined to do. Cf. 1 Thess 5:9; Rom 8:28-30; Eph 1:12; Jude 4.

CHAPTER 30

MEASUREMENT OF THE TEMPLE

In the journey of almost every Freemason, the question comes up as to how big King Solomon's Temple was. As we attempt to answer that question we first must ask where is the information on its size located? It is not found in the Bible or the Torah but is found in what is called the "Massecheth Middoth (Being the Mishnic Tractate Descriptive of the Measurements of the Temple)." This is a Jewish type of commentary on the Torah, Tanach and other Holy writings from the Hebrews. This Middoth contains valuable information on the observance and practices of Judaism. With that in mind, we can explore some of what the Hebrews have written down. I might point out that Rose's Guide to the Temple was based on this description.

We learn from the Tractate that the priests kept watch in the Temple in three places: in the house Avtinas, and in the house Nitsuts, and in the house of Moked; and the Levites in twenty-one places: 5 at the five gates leading into the Temple (the Mountain of the House), 4 in the four angles within, 5 at the five gates of the court, 4 in its four angles without, and 1 in the chamber of offering, and 1 in the chamber of the vail, and 1 behind the Most Holy Place (the House of Atonement). What we see here is that there were guards stationed all over the Temple in strategic locations.[10]

---

[10] https://www.biblestudytools.com/history/edersheim-sketches-jewish-life/appendix-i.html

It also tells us that there were five gates to the Temple enclosure (otherwise known as the Temple Mount): there were two gates of Huldah from the south, which served for entrance and for exit; upon the eastern gate, was a representation of the city of Shushan, and by it the high priest who burned the Red Heifer and went out upon the Mount of Olives. There were seven gates in the court: three on the north, and three on the south, and one in the east. That in the south was the gate of burning; second to it, the gate of the firstborn; third to it, the water gate. That in the east was the gate of Nicanor, and two chambers belonged to it. Each gate had associated with it an appropriate number of chambers and rooms to fit the purpose of whom or what the gate served. Along with the description of the gates were the descriptions of the rooms and what they were used for and how the Priest would close a gate. [11]

From the description we learn that the Temple enclosure (the Temple Mount) was 500 cubits by 500 cubits; it was largest on the south; next largest on the east; then on the north; smallest on the west. All who entered the Temple enclosure entered by the right and turned and went out by the left. All the doorways and gates which were there, were twenty cubits high, and ten cubits wide, except that in the porch. All the doorways which were there, had doors, except that in the porch. All the gates which were there, had lintels, except that in the gate Tadi, which had two stones resting, this on the back of that. All the gates which were there, were renewed to be with gold,

---

[11] https://www.biblestudytools.com/history/edersheim-sketches-jewish-life/appendix-i.html

except the gate of Nicanor, because there was wrought upon them a miracle, and some say, because the brass sparkled.[12]

The Court of the women was 135 cubits long by 135 cubits broad, and four chambers were in the four angles, each 40 cubits square, and they were not roofed in. We also see that there were chambers beneath the Court of Israel, and they opened upon the Court of the Women. It is there the Levites placed their harps, and their psalteries, and their cymbals, and all the musical instruments. The Court of Israel was 135 cubits long by 11 wide, and similarly, the Court of the Priests was 135 long by 11 wide, and the beams divided the Court of Israel and the Court of the Priests.[13]

One of the more interesting facts was that the altar was 32 by 32 [cubits]. In the south-western corner were two apertures, like small nostrils, and the blood, poured on the base to the west, and on the base to the south, descended through them, which co-mingled in the canal, and flowed out into the brook Kedron. The Laver was between the porch and the altar and sloped towards the south. Between the porch and the altar were 22 cubits, and 12 steps were there, each step half a cubit high. The doorway to the porch was 40 cubits high and 20 broad. It goes on to say that five beams of ash were on the top of it; the lowest protruded over the doorway on most sides by a cubit.

In Perek IV or Chapter 4 of the tractate, we read about the entrances to the temple, the number of gates and how they were adorned, the number of chambers on each side for the priest and how they were decorated. It also gave some interesting facts about trap

---

[12] https://www.biblestudytools.com/history/edersheim-sketches-jewish-life/appendix-i.html
[13] https://www.biblestudytools.com/history/edersheim-sketches-jewish-life/appendix-i.html

doors which led to tunnels beneath the temple. I might point out that a winding-stair went up from the north-eastern corner to the north-western corner, by which they went up to the roofs of the chambers. One went up the winding-stair with its face to the west, and went all along the north side, until it came to the west.

But most Masons would be interest to learn that the Sanctuary was 100 by 100, by 100 high; the solid foundation 6 cubits, and the height upon it 40 cubits; 1 cubit, decorated scroll; 2 cubits, the place for the water-droppings; 1 cubit covering, and 1 cubit pavement, and the height of the Alijah 40 cubits, and 1 cubit scroll-work, and 2 cubits the place for the dropping, and 1 cubit covering, and 1 cubit pavement, and 3 cubits balustrade, and 1 cubit scare-raven.

According to the tractate, the walls are arranged as follows: "from the east to the west 100 cubits—the wall of the porch 5, and the porch 11; the wall of the Sanctuary 6, and its interior space 40 cubits, 1-cubit intermediate wall, and 20 cubits the Most Holy Place, the wall of the Sanctuary 6, the little chamber 6, and the wall of the little chamber 5." The walls of the Sanctuary 6, its inner area 20 cubits, the Sanctuary 6, the little chamber 6, the wall of the winding-stair 5, the winding-stair 3, the wall of the little chamber 5, and the wall of the little chamber 6, and the wall of the Sanctuary 6 run from the north to the south 70 cubits.

Finally, in Chapter 5, we learn the whole court was 187 cubits long by 135 cubits wide. From the east to the west 187: the place for the tread of Israel 11 cubits; the place for the tread of the priests 11 cubits; the altar 32; between the porch and the altar 22 cubits; the Sanctuary 100 cubits; and 11 cubits behind the house of Atonement.

We also see that from the north to the south 135 cubits: the altar and the circuit or circumference 62.

So, as we can surmise the temple was huge. A cubit at that time was a mans forearm. Today we calculate it at 18 inches. I urge you to read the original MASSECHETH MIDDOTH

(Being the Mishnic Tractate Descriptive of the Measurements of the Temple) by Rabbi Alfred Edersheim, contained in his work called Sketches in Jewish Life, which can be found on-line and Rose Publishing's Guide to the Temple. Both resources will help to enlighten your journey through Masonry.

For Further Reading:
https://www.biblestudytools.com/history/edersheim-sketches-jewish-life/appendix-i.html the article is by Alfred Edersheim.

ABOUT THE AUTHOR

Right Worshipful Brother Doug Reece

Right Worshipful Brother Doug Reece was raised in St. Louis County, Missouri. Doug graduated from Pattonville Senior High School in 1970 following which he served in the US Air Force in Boise, Idaho from 1972 to 1976. Doug was discharge with the rank of E-4. Doug Graduated from Lael College and Graduate School with a BS in Biblical Studies in 2003 and Graduated from Covington Theological Seminary in 2007 with a Masters in Biblical Studies. He is one of the few that have obtained a Doctorate in Eschatology from Wycliffe Theological Seminary. He and Gayle, who grew up in St. Charles County, were married on October 30, 1993, and have lived in the Kansas City area since 1997.

Doug grew up in a Masonic family where he was a member of Mid-County Chapter of DeMolay and he was inducted into the DeMolay Legion of Honor in 2005. Doug has served as Worshipful Master five times, as District Deputy Grand Master of the 17th District in 2004-05, and as District Deputy Grand Lecturer for the 7th District for 10 years. He was honored to be chosen to serve as Grand Orator in 2013-2014. Doug retired as the Executive Secretary of the St. Joseph Valley of the Scottish Rite after serving 10 years in that capacity. Doug joined both the Scottish Rite and the Shrine in 1973 in St. Louis and transferring to the St. Joseph bodies of both in the early 2000's. Doug and Gayle are members of the Order of the Eastern Star, where they served together as Worthy Matron and Worthy Patron in 2006 and again in 2011. They are also both members of the Order of the Amaranth, having first served as Royal Matron and Patron of Adah Court #1 in 2010-2011. Doug has served as the Grand Prelate of Missouri Grand Court Order of Amaranth for the past several years and served as Grand Royal Patron 2018-2019.

Check out these Masonic books from Perfect Ashlar Publishing

Leading from the East: Innovative Strategies for Masonic Lodges

By Christophor Galloway, PM

For over 200 years, Masonic scholars have written about the need for innovation in Freemasonry to "save our fraternity." Within the pages of Leading From the East, resources and strategies will help Blue Lodge leaders identify their vision, attract new members from several different generations, and engage the new members who join. Additionally, the very same strategies will bring back those Brothers who have disengaged from our Craft. A Worshipful Master implemented the strategies presented in this book at a Blue Lodge that was in jeopardy of closing its doors forever and now that same lodge has a bright future. Finally, this book is also a call to action that Masonic leaders must take a new approach to keep Freemasonry around for another 300 years.

The Profound Pontifications of Big John Deacon, Freemason Extraordinaire

Volume I – IV

By James "Chris" Williams IV, PM

Brother Big John Deacon is a larger-than-life Texas Freemason and Past Master. He towers at 6 feet 7 inches tall and weighs in at 275 pounds. People seem to always notice him in his black alligator boots and 7X Stetson Silverbelly cowboy hat.

He commands attention when he walks into a room with his plain-spoken and exuberant personality. Brother Chris Williams met him several years ago when Brother Deacon's large black F-350 pick-up truck needed repairs. Brother Williams has authentically captured Big John's gruff but gentle cowboy charm and values, which his Masonic membership reinforces. The story of their friendship and adventures is appealing and memorable. Readers may also be familiar with the "Old Tyler's Talks" by Carl H. Claudy, which first appeared in 1921. In many ways, the John Deacon series is a contemporary version of them. Within the pages of each book, there is a pearl of folksy wisdom that is timeless. Brother Deacon is a mix of walking (and mechanical) disasters and knowledge born of passion and profound reflections on Freemasonry and today's Lodge challenges.

The John Deacon book series will have readers laughing, crying, and, more importantly, reflecting on Freemasonry.

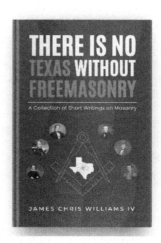

There is No Texas Without Freemasonry: A Collection of Short Writings on Masonry

By James "Chris" Williams IV, PM

Within the covers of this book is a collection of Masonic papers written over the last twenty-five years by Brother Williams. Most of them have been presented at various Masonic and non- Masonic gatherings. There is No Texas Without Freemasonry is the first and most famous paper presented to date by Brother Williams. This book is an excellent addition to any Masonic library.

Each chapter is short enough to be read as an education piece in the Lodge or as the focus of family education night. Enjoy each page as you laugh, cry, and, more importantly, reflect on Freemasonry.

Light Reflections: Philosophical Thoughts and Observations of a Texas Freemason

By Bradley E. Kohanke, PM

Freemasonry in the United States was arguably at its peak during the decade following the first World War. The Masonic writings of the day were eloquent, easy to read, concise, and filled with thought-provoking opinions and observations. This was the model after which Bradley E. Kohanke patterned his writings. For nearly 10 years, Brother Kohanke, a Past Master, former District Deputy Grand Master, and former Grand Orator for the Grand Lodge of Texas wrote a monthly article for his Lodge's newsletter.

Also included are his Orations from the Texas Grand Lodge Historical Observances in 2019 and his Grand Oration from the Grand Annual Communication in January of 2020. As Brother Kohanke puts it:

Masonry holds no secrets or sacred knowledge that are suddenly revealed to the initiate. Rather, it provides a framework on which to build…a guide for living. It offers a way to attain that knowledge over time through learning, patience, and truth. And it does so without harming others in their search. This practice of perfecting one's self is ancient beyond record and is the true measure of success. The attainment of balance in one's life…achieving happiness with yourself, without interfering with the happiness of others, and proactively helping others in their search for balance in their lives…that is success.

It is a noble quest, the objective of which can only truly be obtained by those who are worthy and true…to themselves and each other. Good luck on your quest, and enjoy it.

"Masonic duty is to learn and to teach others."

Brotherhood of God:

A Book of Masonic Prayers

By Garron C. Daniels

Brotherhood of God is a collection of prayers to be used by Freemasons, used both within the Lodge and in daily life. It is an aid for the spiritual needs of the Fraternity to remind all of the importance of God in all that we do.

Garron C. Daniels is a Freemason from the State of Missouri. He's a member of Brotherhood Lodge #269 in St Joseph, Mo, a member of the Scottish Rite and York Rite, and several other fundraising bodies of Freemasonry.

He gains his influence in writing from his studies about the Fraternity as well as his studies in becoming an Episcopal Priest at the University of the South: School of Theology. He continues to dedicate his time to exploring the religious aspects of Masonry and where Christianity plays a role in it.

Devotion To St. Constantine the Great:
Emperor, Convert, and Devout Follower of Christ
By Garron C. Daniels

Emperor Constantine the Great is a figure that some throughout history have deemed controversial. Yet, his significance and conversion to Christianity have impacted the faith in ways we will never fully understand. While he was a flawed sinner like any other, he still was the primary force that helped bring Christianity from an oppressed faith to being the religion of the Empire. Constantine was truly a Saintly figure who lived to serve not just as an Emperor but as a mere servant to the Almighty.

**A MASON'S JOURNEY – NOAH'S QUEST
VOLUME III: "FAITHFUL CRAFTSMAN"**

Because of this, we must seriously and sincerely believe that Emperor Constantine the Great should be considered St Constantine, an emperor, convert, and a devout follower of Christ.

A Masons Journey – Noah's Quest:
Volume I: Trial at the Gate
By William Boyd

A Mason's Journey – Noah's Quest" Volume I, Trial at the Gate," is a fictional look at a masonic journey, and it is unusual because it starts at an unexpected point in a mason's journey. It is an introduction to Brother Noah Lewis as he reconciles the books of his life and discovers the unseen forces at work, guiding him along his journey. Above all, it contextualizes and illustrates some of the ideas and concepts the author has believed and have described in a variety of other non-fiction vehicles and may, perhaps, be the first in a series intended to animate the tenets of freemasonry through the fictional quest of Brother Noah Lewis. We all have beliefs about our call to accountability and how we may ultimately learn the value of our labors.

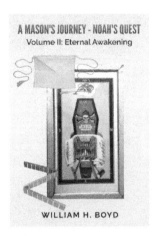

A Masons Journey – Noah's Quest:
Volume II: Eternal Awakening
By Bill Boyd

In book two of the series Noah has come upon The Gate, he had been presented with poignant scenes that were steeped in meaning and were obviously intended to impact him in certain ways. But there was so much he still did not know about this reality and what, if any, control he held. He did not know if or how he should interact with these scenes as they unfolded around him. And he did not know if the scenes were real. Or maybe they were allegories for events from his life gone by? Perhaps they are intended to represent new lessons, meant to teach him further lessons?

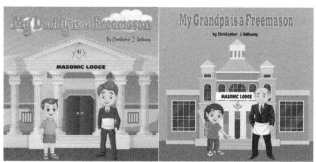

Share Freemasonry with Future Generations with These Childrens Books

By

Christophor J. Galloway

Made in the USA
Monee, IL
04 August 2023

40406893R00132